Human Consciousness, Mental System and Mental Self

Human Consciousness, Mental System and Mental Self

Thoughts, Beliefs, Attitudes and Excitements

Rokneddin Darvish Ph.D.

ISBN-13: 9781533444677
ISBN-10: 1533444676

*To my beautiful and loyal wife Susan
and my gentle sons Babak and Siamak Darvish
for their compassion, patience, and inspirations*

Table of Contents

About the Author

Rokneddin Darvish, Ph. D is a licensed behavior specialist in the State of Utah at present. He has received his BA in English language and literature and social sciences from the University of Tehran, MS in sociology and psychology from the Texas A&I University, Ph. D in sociology, social organization and disorganization from North Texas State University (now University of North Texas), and a Certification Degree in School Psychology from University of Utah. His work history includes: working with Juvenile Delinquents at State School in Texas for 3 years, Inmates at Utah State Prison for 5 years and performed psychological services for individuals with developmental disabilities, autism and mental illness for 21 years at Utah State Developmental Center, and the Utah State Prison in Utah. Population he served includes Individuals with developmental disability, mental illness and criminal behaviors as well as students with behavior problems in schools and older population in care centers.

Dr. Darvish worked in different capacities including Behavior Specialist/Analyst Consultant, Program Support Supervisor, Caseworker II, Dorm Director, Dean of Faculty, President and Executive Director of University. In addition he provided behavioral services for total of 26 years as a Ph. D behavior specialist/analyst and BC III (Behavior consultant III) working with individuals with Autism, developmental disabilities and individuals with mental illness in different communities in Utah. He retired from the State of Utah on July, 2010.

Dr. Darvish presented many topics in the area of developmental disability, mental illness and behavior analysis at various professional conferences and completed several research projects and coauthored several articles published in the behavior analytic and scientific journals in the United States of America.

Preface

In this book I have tried to show the influence of consciousness on the positive side of our existence and mental system as a realm of hell and mental self as the source of the evil. It also reflects Rumi's philosophy and ideas as related to the topic. I have tried to analyze Rumi's ideas from a sociological and psychological perspective. Rumi's poems are poems and messages of human conversion from immature mental self to the real, objective self or consciousness. This book also includes Rumi's recommendations about the methods of conversion such as patience, silence, relaxation, and acceptance of the events and incidents of this moment without reaction, resistance and judgement. The nature of acceptance is total acceptance without fighting against the event or incident of this moment, and consciously surrendering to the universal consciousness. Rumi's ideas have stimulated and created a new synthesis of ideas and knowledge in my mind. What Rumi tried to present to all human beings is the art of living and loving. Rumi's poems, philosophy and ideas make us to come alive and comprehend who we really are? What our responsibilities are? And how we can rejoin our source?

According to Rumi, we should experience the unconditional love instead of conditional and selfish love. We can only really become aware of another person's essence by falling in love with that person. If there is a real unconditional love, then, it is the universal consciousness trapped in one person's body falling in love with itself as a consciousness in another person's body. In this case the physical sexual attraction is only a small part of a greater spiritual attraction of consciousness in two separate bodies which is an eternal love. But when a mental self falls in love with another mental self it is not real love but only a short lived passion and sexual physical attraction. Along with love of life, Rumi emphasizes on the recognition and awareness of human being of universal consciousness which resides within us and constantly working through us and helps us to free ourselves of the dark prison of mental system by deactivating and finally dissolving our mental self or internal evil. We can escape all these pain and sufferings by being patient and unconditionally accepting our situation.

Rumi's ideas of unity and interconnectedness of everything and all parts and particles of the universe as well as evolution of consciousness from the solids to plants and animals and finally human beings are highly impressing. His notion that it is within human mind that consciousness continue to evolve and after reaching to a certain maturity level and gaining enough experiences as related to the external world and when the time is right and ripe, freedom of consciousness from our mental system and returning and rejoining the universal consciousness becomes possible. This idea provided me with a grand theory of existence, evolution of consciousness and the final destination. Rumi's ideas of the human and the universe and human's position in the universe, answered all my questions regarding the main question of human philosophy trying to answer where we came from, why we are here and where we are heading to in the future.

Rumi's ideas helped me to understand that all our human pains and suffering relates to our pain addicting mental self with limited knowledge as an internal evil and the biased mental system with limited capacity as an internal hell which is unidimensional and works only through duality and comparing and contrasting two opposites or complementary phenomena. His example of mental self only concentrating on the psychological time and that living in the past and becoming depressed as related to the negative events and incidents of the past and becoming anxious and worried as related to the probable events and incidents of the future, is good explanation of two major emotional and psychological problems of human beings. Mental system and mental self by emphasizing on either the past or the present are influenced by distorted mental concepts which do not have any real basis in reality. Escaping from the real time of the present and this moment, not letting human to concentrate on the business of the present does not let us enjoy life to the maximum possible level.

Another major influence of Rumi on my family and I, is his emphasize on the real value of being patient, accepting the events as they are happening and not to react impulsively to any event, incident, situation or condition, and surrendering to the universal consciousness. Any form of reaction to any event or situation, can only make our trouble worse and makes mental self, stronger and causes major problem in our daily life. The more reaction we show to different events and situations, the more solid our mental self becomes. I can see a major positive change in my life and my family life by following Rumi's ideas and his formulas of better thinking, feeling and acting and his main theme of concentrating on the art of living and loving. Zoroaster the first prophet of Persia, five thousand years ago emphasized on the good thought, good deed and good action as the main conditions of healthy and normal human life. Thus, our joy and happiness can be achieved if we surrender to the universal consciousness or God which is nothing but light energy and consciousness full of life energy of joy and happiness.

In chapter I and II I tried to explain the main ideas of Rumi regarding mental system and mental self, how we can control and deactivate our mental self and the development of mental self within human mental system. In chapter III, I elaborated on the evolution of consciousness and the mental self within human mental system with an emphasis on the difference between the mental system and the universal consciousness. Chapter IV and V Include positive function of mental system and mental self (ego) and the negative functions and major characteristics of mental system and mental self and considers mental system and mental self as sources of negative excitements, emotions and cognitive distortions and thinking errors. Chapter VI – explains universal consciousness and love: A source of happiness and joy as well as universal consciousness as God and world of unity as paradise: A source of happiness and joy. Chapter VII – concentrates on mental self and artificial love and concept of mental self as evil and mental system as hell: A source of sadness and depression.

Rumi's teachings in poem form, using stories and historical events and figures who are known to most people and examples of everything in the natural world including the sky with milky way, all the solar systems, planets, suns, moons and stars as well as ocean, sea, lake, mountains, rivers, forests, seasons, deserts, humans, animals, plants, solids and the natural processes of evolution, rejuvenation of everything and constant dynamic change, makes it easy for most people to understand what he is trying to teach about our origin, the laws of life, the vine of life and the power of love which holds everything together in the universe. Through his poems, Rumi takes us to a wonderful travel of life and gives us a tour of the real life situations and events. "The general theme of Rumi's thought, is essentially that of the concept of "Tawhid," union with his beloved (The primal root) from which/whom he has been cut off and became aloof, and his longing and desire to restore it." (http://enwiki-pedia.org/wiki/Rumi).

Jalal-e-din Mohammad Molavi Rumi was born in 1207 BC at Balkh in the north-eastern provinces of Persia (Present day Afghanistan) to a Persian speaking family. Rumi worked as a professor in the famous Madrasah at Konya at the age of Twenty-four years. He was highly influenced by Shams-e-Tabrizi, a masterpiece of wisdom. He died in 1273 at Konya (Present day Turkey). Major works completed by Rumi are: 1. Divan-e-Shams-e-Tabrizi (Divan-e- Kabir), 2. Masnavi-e- Ma'navi the best known work of Rumi, and he himself defined his work as a work of the destruction of the worldly for the sake of embracing the Divine.-, and 3. Fihe-Ma-Fih, a collection of mystical sayings (Iran Chamber Society). Rumi's ideas, poems and scholarly works have been translated into several languages and positively affected many people across the world.

Acnowledgements

I wish to acknowledge the major contributions of Mr. Parviz Shahbazi who dedicated his life and productive time trying to introduce Rumi's Poems, works, Philosophy of life and loving, and many other Persian poets, philosophers, and mystics through a TV program called "The Treasure of Presence" and his deep analysis of the selected poems of Rumi. Mr. Shahbazi's interpretation of Rumi's poems had impressed me. His encouragement for Persian language speaking individuals to translate Rumi's work to other languages and to introduce them to the world was also a major motivating factor. I have been motivated by Mr. Shahbazi to write this book to introduce a drop within the vast ocean of Rumi's works and his philosophy of life, and the art of living and loving and laws of life. I have included the sources of joy and tranquility and the sources of sadness in human life. I wrote this book in English language to introduce Rumi's ideas to the English language speaking people, utilizing a psychological and sociological approach. Rumi's works has been translated into many languages by many scholars, but my work is an analysis of Rumi's works using a psychological and sociological point of view. There are hundreds of other Persian poets, philosophers that need to be introduced to the World and I hope other people could engage in this type of scholarly endeavor.

My main acknowledgement is to the Rumi himself for his dedication to vitalize, awaken and transcend human to the highest level of spiritual joy and enlightenment through his works, poems and ideas containing his message of love that speaks directly to the heart of anyone who try to be in contact with. Familiarity and understanding of Rumi's philosophy of life and love, gives anyone a sense of inspiration and self-appreciation to know that all human have the same universal consciousness within them and to consider themselves as precious beings. Knowing that consciousness is the real essence of all humans and resides within all forms also gives a real meaning to the objective unity among all human beings and the universe.

Rumi's emphasize on the awareness and recognition of our internal consciousness that is an extension of the universal consciousness and a source of joy, tranquility and creativity as opposed to our mental system and mental self that is a source of all human evil including our miseries, negative thoughts, beliefs, opinions, customs, rites, excitements and emotions is highly awakening. It is our mental system and mental self that is causing all our physical and emotional pains and suffering. Rumi uses many stories and religious and historical events to help people to remember the stories, but his real intension is to teach the meanings behind the stories, symbols, metaphors and similes.

I

Introduction
Human Consciousness, Mental System
and Mental Self (Ego)

*"To be or not to be is not my dilemma. To break away from both worlds is not bravery. To be unaware of the wonders that exist in me, that is real madness!" (Rumi,13ᵗʰ Century))
(Translated by Mafi & Kolin, P. 48)*

Mental system is composed of many dimensions or subsystems including thoughts, beliefs, ideas, opinions, emotions and excitements. A combination of different dimensions of mental system and our physical system produces our mental self. Our mental self is an ever-changing phenomenon, constantly changing according to the social and environmental situations, incidents and events. When an incident occurs, a situation or condition arises that we define it negatively, our mental self immediately react to the those incidents, situation or conditions without using our neocortex the upper brain and consequently we engage in an inappropriate behavior or take a wrong course of action. Most human problems and deviant, illegal, immoral and criminal behaviors relate to our immediate, impulsive and unthoughtful reaction that is done by our mental self. We are so involved in our daily activity and trying to concentrate on worldly matters and attractions of the external world that we forget our internal spiritual values and dimension that are main basis and goals of our existence. In his poem called "the right use of forms," Rumi called the universal consciousness, the universal soul which has connection to partial soul of human being.

Individual mental self (ego) is being established throughout our life and controls our behavior at any moment. A collectivity of mental selves establishes the social group mental self that is considered the great mental self or ego. An individual mental self is always under control and influence of collective social mental selves. An individual mental self, imitates and copies what social or group mental self is doing or dictating through its formal and informal rules and codes of conduct. It is the social group mental self that is responsible for all the major conflicts and wars among different nations, religions, and ethnic groups. To Rumi, our mental system is equivalent of the dark prison and hell within us and our mental self is representative of evil within full of negative and destructive ideas, thoughts, beliefs, opinions and desires about material world, other people and belongings within the external world. We have two types of souls or life. One is our real, objective universal consciousness and the other is the temporary life of our mental self that is a reflection and picture of our real self. The co-identification with external world produces a cover between our mental self and the real self or consciousness.

Rumi believes that there is a relationship between our universal consciousness and physical and mental consciousness. The universal consciousness penetrates into forms including human forms. Part of the universal consciousness gets separated from the total consciousness and goes into form and creates our physical and mental consciousness within the mental system where a mental self will be established later. Our mental self, become co-identified and codependent with the material and mental forms and things, however, realizes that forms such as our thought, beliefs, opinions and ideas as well as material things can't give us real living life. Our physical and mental growth is the beginning and a vehicle of our spiritual growth in human form. This is because total consciousness needs to experience the world and become mature within human body and mental system and experience the pain and suffering of being separated from the source. Being separated from the source the consciousness that is trapped within the mental system, becomes thirsty of rejoining the source. Life will determine when and at what point we are ready to be free from the cold prison of our mental system. Thus, at any moment human being has to search for the real meaning in his/her life to transcend the external world and detach itself from it.

After universal consciousness goes into our mental system, and physical system, it turns into physical and mental consciousness which becomes temporarily unaware of its source or origin and become co-identified and attached to the worldly things. The consciousness is alien in human form or body particularly within mental system and to the mental self, but is friend and familiar with spiritual, real, objective and original self. To Rumi the mental system or hell and mental self or evil are functional and under control of God or universal consciousness and are two states of our internal existence. The formless universal consciousness and everything that relate to it represents the heaven and our mental system represents the hell. The main agent of mental system or hell is the evil of mental self with its pain producing tendencies and activities. The joy of every moment for us is to suppress our mental self or ego, the representative of evil and instead to become unified with consciousness. We have two choices either to control the evil of mental self or ego or to be controlled by it which is disturbing and damaging to us. When we consider ourselves separated from universal consciousness and use the language of our mental system that is based on duality, then we think about "we" versus God or universal consciousness as two separate beings. But in fact, we are consciousness or God within our own physical and mental system.

To Rumi, we struggle to get out of our form, mental system and mental self to search for a real meaning in our life. This is because we became separated and away from our source or consciousness. In order to experience a rich life of spirituality, love and finding a real meaning in our life, we should be able to free ourselves out of our evil mental system and mental self which constantly creates variety of pains in the forms of sadness, anger and destruction. We should rejoin and be united with our source or consciousness. In line with Rumi, Victor Frankl (1998) in his book called "The Man's Search for Meaning," stated that the main motivation for human being is to stay alive and survive in the worst condition or situation by concentrating on love and search for meaning in our life. He talks about the Jews who became imprisoned in Auschwitz concentration camp for years as an example and showed that those who survived in that camp were motivated by a need to search for real meaning and love in their lives. Frankl believes that a search for meaning is part of the essence of our human spirit and essential for our survival. He offers "Logotherapy as a means of searching for the meaning of the existence of human and human's search for the meaning in his/her life" (1998, p. 121). We can reach to a meaning in life both with and without struggle, but it would be more ideal if we can reach to a real meaning in life through concentration on our real self and consciousness. Human consciousness is swimming within the ocean of the meanings toward the realm of unity. Thus we should not consider this world as our home and stay as a stranger within this limited space of our mental system that reflects a picture of the world.

Rumi believes that human consciousness came from a long trip going through solids, plants, and animals, and now is within human body and mental system. Being within our mental system and act as a mental self, we only create pain, destruction and suffering for ourselves. We should not be away, separated or unaware of our origin or consciousness at any time. Our security comes from our closeness to our origin or our real self within us. Our thoughts, beliefs, opinions, excitements are very shallow but our real essence the consciousness is deep within us and control our mental self and our destiny in the long run. Mental self, tries to resist against our internal consciousness and wishes to become independent from our consciousness, but this is not possible. Our internal evil or mental self constantly creates pain and suffering and our consciousness neutralizes its deviant actions. Our mental and physical consciousness can't relax in human body and is restless to free itself from the prison of mental system.

The mental self as an artificial being lives in a fantasy house that is constantly wearing off and even when mental self tries to repair it, it does not last long. Mental self constantly steals life force within human body to use it in a deviant way. The mental self creates a sense of existence and is familiar with death thus, is in a constant fear of losing its transitory and artificial existence. The consciousness of presence has strong hands that holds the leash of our mental self and stop it from making trouble for us. Mental self always lives in an imaginary house of thoughts and beliefs. If we destroy one house, mental self tries to build another one, and always jumps from one thought to the next and is not able to rest and be quiet. There is only one life that lives within and without everything and variety of all forms and creatures in the world. Life always gives us messages and talks to us but we try to ignore those messages and instead let our mental self, misbehave. Problem with mental self is that it chooses the material and non-material things that are part of the external world as his/her friends and tries to be aware of self through attachment with objects or thoughts, beliefs and ideas. To expect to receive life from non-livings is work without pay and waste of time.

To Rumi it is the mental self who initiates the behavior within our mental system and then, our physical body makes the move to engage and complete the behavior. The initiation of thought in our mind is the obsession and the behavior that occurs by our physical system is the compulsion part of the behavior. While our mental self who is addicted to pain and suffering tries to get us into trouble, our real, objective self or universal consciousness prohibits us to do so. Our physical body moves and takes action based on the impulsive reaction of mental self that is why most of our behaviors are uncalculated and unacceptable. Our real, objective self and consciousness constantly control the behavior of our mental self. Similarly, Skinner (1953, p. 284) believes that, "the organism behaves, while the self, initiates or directs behavior. Moreover, more than one self is needed to explain the behavior of one organism... But there appears to be two selves acting simultaneously and in different ways when one self, controls another or is aware of the activity of another. " Freud's concepts of "Id," "ego" and "Super-ego" are three different parts of self or personality which also are acting in different ways. The id is present from the birth and works based on instincts. While ego tries to engage in inappropriate behavior based on our negative emotions, the "Super-ego," tries to control the "ego" and stop the behavior (1923). Freud's concept of "ego" is equivalent of Rumi's concept of mental self and his concept of "superego" is equivalent of Rumi's concept of real self or consciousness.

While, Skinner considers external social and physical environmental exigencies and history of reinforcement of an individual as responsible factors for individual's behavior and states that "the self is most commonly used as hypothetical cause of action. So long as external variable go unnoticed or ignored, their function is assigned to an originating agent within the organism. If we cannot show what is responsible for a man's behavior, we say that he himself is responsible for it," (Skinner, 1953. P.283), Rumi believes as human being with intelligence, reason and logic and power of analyzing any situation, we have freedom of choice to choose between appropriate and inappropriate behavior, however, due to the nature of our mental self which is made of our negative thoughts, beliefs and excitements and co-identification with pains and sufferings and its tendency to react impulsively, to resist and to fight, we engage in uncalculated abnormal behaviors. Rumi reminds us that we have a choice to choose between our deviant and destructive mental self and our constructive real, objective self or consciousness. Rumi emphasizes that no one or nothing out there in the external world is responsible for our behavior. We are responsible for our behavior and it is our internal evil of mental self that decides to engage in inappropriate behavior if we let that to happen. Thus evil does not come from external environment but works from within human beings.

Skinner also believes that emotions are not responsible for our behaviors. He says, "The "emotions" are excellent examples of the fictional causes to which we commonly attribute behavior. We run away because of "fear" and strike because of "Anger"; we are paralyzed by "rage" and depressed by "grief." These causes are in turn attributed to events in our history of present circumstances--to the things which frighten or engage or make us angry or sad (Skinner, 1953, p.160). Unlike Skinner, Rumi believes that thought, belief and excitement or emotion would not directly make us to engage in a behavior or action. It is the mental self as an evil agent of mental system with all negative thoughts, beliefs, excitements that as an artificial transitory self within our mental system which initiates the behavior and our physical system moves and perform the behavior. Thus, we should not let our mental self which is automatic and impulsive to create excessive pain and suffering for us. Instead we should let our real self or consciousness works through us to provide us with the correct guidelines and plan of action.

Rumi considers mental system and mental self as scarecrow or the head of a dead animal that farmers used in the field to frighten the birds and animals from destroying the crops or fruits. With this example Rumi tries to teach us that anything that frightens us in this world is the symbol of scarecrows or the head of dead animals which are dead with no life force within them. Thus, why we should be afraid of artificial objects and worldly things when we are formless consciousness? Fear is only from the unknown phenomena. The mental self does not have a balance in life, either wants to live forever which is not possible or to die and not to suffer and bear the constant pain and suffering. The death of our mental self is to come alive with life and consciousness. Human has suffered from the disease and pains of our mental self for a long time. When we get out of our mental self we gain our physical, mental and psychological health. Our mental system is very limited and has a beginning and end, while our consciousness does not have any limit. Within the mental system, we as mental self are separate from the universal consciousness due to the duality of our mental system, that has to have two opposites to compare, but within the realm of unity, we are united and complementary with each other and with our origin.

Rumi uses Pharaoh of Egypt as a major example of mental self or evil within human mental system. Pharaoh is made up of a woven texture of co-identification, codependency and attachment to the material life of this world as well as exaggerated distorted, negative and disturbing thought, beliefs, opinions, and excitements. Pharaoh is not just one individual but a negative force within all Pharaoh like people. Pharaoh appears in a negative form of energy and pain that destroy and enslave thousands of people. Pharaoh has a representative within the mental system of every human being. Pharaoh has a parasitic life which gets its nutrition from our positive energy and turns it into a negative destructive energy. The main Pharaoh is the collective mental system of society which controls and misleads all individual mental selves. We should be aware of our own individual Pharaoh and the great Pharaoh which creates all the human pain and sufferings. Pain and suffering we receive from our internal Pharaoh is one form of experience and a major sign of something bigger and deeper problem within us. Pain and suffering is an indicator of greater abnormalities within our mental system of thought, belief, opinion and excitements. We consider all these pains and suffering as a means of providing us with awareness and recognition of our internal pain producing Pharaoh.

We may not try to eliminate all types of pains and sufferings that we or our family members are experiencing, because all these pains and sufferings are giving us more experience of major abnormalities within our mental system which is performed by our confused and distorted mental self. Our beauty is within our internal consciousness, not our physical appearance, color, shape of our body. Instead of looking at the mirror to see our face and body and try to make ourselves look better as we perceive, we should use a spiritual mirror to see and observe our internal pain and be aware of what causes our internal pain. It is the universal consciousness that operates and plans the life of humans the best way possible. As Rumi believes, the worst event can be the best event in our life in the long run. Moses is a symbol of treasure of presence who, came to eliminate the source of pain or Pharaoh's great evil mental self. Pharaoh had major internal pain and would transfer all his pains to the people of Egypt particularly Jewish people. Moses became the mirror of light to show Pharaoh of his internal evil. Moses's snake eating Pharaoh's snakes is a symbol of Moses consciousness from the realm of unity swallowing Pharaoh's mental self or evil.

Rumi uses the story of the Life of Moses and Pharaoh as an example to show that the worst event can turn into the best event under life planning of universal consciousness. Most events or accidents may look undesirable at first, but if we be patient and do not react to those event, we will see that consciousness has a plan for us and the same events that we perceived as negative one, may turn to a productive one. Pharaoh had a dream that a baby will be born and raised in Egypt who will be the enemy of the Pharaoh and destroy him in the future. Based on his dream he decided to engage in a criminal behavior of ordering the killing of all the new born of Egyptian families. During the same night that Pharaoh was planning and ordering for all the new born children of Egypt to be killed, Moses mother put him in a basket and put the basket in the Nile River. Moses then, arrived to Pharaoh's castle through the River Nile as a baby and start growing up in Pharaoh's mansion and dynasty only to turn against him later and try to change him for the better. The grand work of consciousness was in process to destroy the Pharaoh from within his own dynasty. Pharaoh's fear and dream turned into his worst nightmare. The worst fear of Pharaoh tuned into the best situation for Moses to become part of Pharaoh's family and then to try to save the Jewish people who were enslaved, from their long time slavery under despotic government of Pharaoh.

Rumi declares that Pharaoh gave humans poison to drink and put them under the evil Talisman and created intense pain for them to suffer and that is the nature of the great evil or the mental system. Even from the time of Adam and Eve our evil mental system or mental self the internal representative of evil forced Adam and Eve to use their mental self and see their limited world through the dark glasses of their mental system which misled them to become co-identified and attached to the things of this world and to their biased thought, belief, opinions and excitements. This was the first perceived sin of Adam and Eve as the representative and ancestors of all human beings. Rumi informs all humans that now human spring is under way and it is the time of rejuvenation and revitalization and the party of the nature with the musical sounds of nature and moment of reaching to the treasure of presence for all creatures of the universe. Human presence can be achieved by jumping out of the prison of mental system by dissolving our mental self. The plants and vegetation reach to their presence through seeding, flowering and opening their buds and repeating their life cycles. Animals reach to their presence by procreating their own species and repeating the cycle of life. Solids will reach their presence when they turn into gems, diamonds, gold and silver which radiate the light energy toward all directions. This is glorification and presence of dirt and stones through conversion to something valuable.

Rumi refers to the Noah as a symbol of consciousness and Noah's arch as the realm of unity. Those who listened to Noah's recommendations and came to the realm of unity were safe. Even pairs of animals were safe. However, for those including Noah's son who did not believe the Noah and refused to come to the realm of unity within Noah's ship were perished in the water. One of the major problem those people had was that they were people who were imprisoned in their mental system and this turned them to rigid mental selves. Their wrong pride stopped them from listening to the Noah. When Noah tells his son to come into the ship, he tells his father that "I go to the top of the mountain where water could not reach me." The mountain to Rumi stands for the mountain of mental system. The disobeying the consciousness was the main reason for the people including: Canaan, Noah's son to die. Then, the water covered everywhere including the top of the mountain and drowned all of those mental selves. The universal consciousness has the right plan for us. But if we resist against the flow of consciousness and fight against it we lose. The same way if we swim against the current in the river, even if we are the best swimmer, we will finally get exhausted and give up and lose.

Rumi tells the story of Joseph and Jacob the Prophets in the poem form. He considers joseph and Jacob as symbols of people who have reached the presence of consciousness or God. Kanaan, where the two prophets lived is considered a symbol of the realm of unity. Joseph brothers were the symbols of mental selves. The well that Joseph's brothers throw him in, is a symbol of the well of mental system and Egypt is considered a symbol of this world. Zuleika, the wife of the prime minister of Egypt is considered the symbol of passion. The coins that Joseph brothers received from the people of the caravan to sell Joseph as a slave, is considered the symbol of the material belongings. Rejoining of Joseph to his father Jacob at the end of the story is symbol of Joseph returning to the realm of unity. Joseph accepting and forgiving his brothers who were mental selves is symbol of consciousness or God forgiving the mental selves and also a symbol of repentance of Joseph brothers returning to consciousness or God. The blindness of Zuleika after Joseph rejected her is a symbol of mental self being blinded by her passion and mental self. And ability for Zuleika to see again is a symbol of God or consciousness opening her spiritual eyes to see the reality. This story is very long but very educational. It teaches us about the consciousness as God and light force that brightens and leads the whole universe and that mental system as hell and mental self as an evil constantly misleads and seduces us to engage in wrong doings.

Rumi believes that we would not be able to become alive and experience the living life, before we sacrifice our mental self or ego. The same way that seeds of the plants have to go to their grave under the dirt and be dissolved and sacrificed themselves in order to produce hundreds of new seeds. Thus, no seed goes into the ground without producing hundreds of new seeds and this is the cycle of life and reproduction of new life. Silk worm eats a lot of leafs and become fat and big only to be sacrificed and when the time is ready to burst and open up its belly to let the new form of life which is butterfly to fly into the air. Another form of sacrifice is the salmon fish which travels for miles with a lot of efforts to reach the highest ground rivers possible only to spread its eggs in the safe area of the river and then dies. But with sacrificing each salmon's life thousands of new salmons or new forms of life appears which go back to the ocean or sea and lakes and the cycle begins again. The energy of life continuously flows through us and we are observer at this moment and see how the energy of joy, creativity, tranquility radiates from us toward everything.

To Rumi, being born is becoming free from the limited and temporary world of the mother's womb to a second temporary but bigger external world. But this time, consciousness goes into a new limited and temporary space of our mental system. Next stage is the sacrifice of our mental system and obtaining our freedom by joining the universal consciousness. Rumi uses the story of Moses in the Mount Saini, when Moses asked God or consciousness to show itself, God appeared as light and fire on the tree, a pure energy and universal consciousness, Moses observing what happened, which was that part of Mount Saini exploded, he passed out. The explosion of Mount Saini is symbol of the explosion and destruction of Moses mental system and experiencing the presence of God as consciousness, energy and fire. Thus physical, mental consciousness was converted to the universal consciousness in Moses. When we get rid of a sense of existence of mental self, life begins to vibrate and dance within all parts of our body, we will be awaken and get tuned with the music of life and dance in line with the dance of the universe or what Rumi calls "Sama." Consciousness comes alive in human form and appears like human but deep down it is life. The whole Universe with all the creatures who live in it is in a constant process of evolution and change. Consciousness within all forms is trying to become alive to its essence.

Mental self, experiences what is considered as happiness and sadness, however both are mental concepts and perceptions relative to the individual mental self and different situations. Happiness and sadness are two sides of the same coin. Sadness can turn into happiness and happiness can turn into sadness at any moment. When we are happy the consciousness within us is operating and when we are sad our mental self is working. That is why the same incident or event that makes someone happy makes another person unhappy or the same incident or event that makes someone happy at one moment may make him/her unhappy in another moment. It is not the incident or event which makes us happy or sad. It is our own internal response to the same event or incident at different point in time which is always this moment. When we are sad it is because our mental self pulls a mask over our universal consciousness which is nothing but joy and happiness. Thus our sadness is the result of not being able to experience happiness. Our main prayer is to be patient and surrendering to our consciousness. Any request or wish that is based on cursing someone or wanting and desiring something of this world is a wrong type of prayer. Complains, prayer and needs of mental self are false and useless.

Rumi believes that we do not need our individual mental self or social mental self to be connected to the universal consciousness. We should use our real objective self which is made of consciousness to relate to the universal consciousness. Mental self, values to the external world and material things and becomes attached to them. We should be able to observe our mental self and catch it in action and put the light on it to clearly see what type of distortion is being used by it. We should constantly be aware of our mental self and deviant plans that our mental self makes to get us into trouble. As soon as we catch our mental self in action, we have opportunity to stop it from taking a wrong course of action. Our universal consciousness, constantly provide us with the recognition and awareness to be able to stop our mental self from engaging in an inappropriate behavior. Mental self is distorted and see everything through dark and polluted glasses. Mental self has a false sense of identification, false values and false prestige and status and has a tendency for false consumption and desiring things as much as possible.

Universal consciousness has penetrated into our physical system in a form-less state and is within us and leads our thought, logic, reason and action. As consciousness we are ascending through the column of light to join our light source or universal consciousness. However, this can only happen, if we live at this moment and not being imprisoned in the psychological time of the past or future. Life is our friend and if it is happening as an event it should not be unpleasant to us. If we try to be patient and accept the event and remain at the service of life, it will work productively through us. The rain shower of life should pour over us to revitalize us and keep us lively. We should learn from the experiences of people who have reached a high level of enlightenment which helps us to become free and independent. Being under the support of life will bring us joy and happiness. However, something that we possess in the external world will make us happy today but, will makes us very sad when we lose it.

Rumi says that the strangest thing is that how consciousness that can't be contained or can't be seen within forms resides within human physical and mental system. A human who has strong and an active mental self, has a rigid thinking and is not made of tenderness. Human consciousness is a stranger in this world because it came from the formless realm of unity into human form. Thus, human feel as a stranger in a temporary world and is rare species due to his/her existence and essence of humanness and godliness. Human is happiness of both world and extension of the life of all creatures. Human is stability and calmness of all hearts. Thus, human existence is not enough. The essence of "to be" need to be experienced and need to turn into "to become" through active struggle. Within the mental systems all humans are separated alienated from each other and from the consciousness within them. But within the realm of unity all humans and the universal consciousness are united. We should wake up of our sleep within our mental system and join our origin. To be present at the life of this moment is the connection between "to be" and "to become" or "to do."

Consciousness is the experiencer. Experience is connected to other experiences. Experience is a thought made possible in our mind as related to our action through interconnection of our senses, nervous system and the brain working together to produce the thought. Our awareness of the events and incidents of the external world using our senses and mental system in combination provides thought within our mental system. Since thought is occurring non-stop and continuously we may get lost within our thought processes. Each experience is passing quickly for example getting angry, getting upset, or sad has a short moment and will be experienced by us. Thus, we should not become involved and lost in these processes of experience. We should only use our mental system for evaluation and obtaining knowledge about our environment and other people to become functional in our life. Using our mental system to engage in perseverative and negative thought process and developing pain and suffering is the negative function of our mental system. Thus we have to shut down our mental system when it does not serve a positive function. The same way that we can't find our way in the dark night, we will not be able to find our way in the dark night of our mental system. Thus, we have to get out of our dark mental system and use the daylight of our consciousness to find our way.

Rumi addresses all human beings who came to this world and they don't know why they are here. He says that human is like an eagle that a heavy weight is attached to his legs and can't fly. But human has to take of the weight and fly high. We are the final product of evolution, consciousness becomes pure in us and improvement comes from within toward outside our system not the other way. When dirt gets separated from the mud, pure water stays on the top separated from the mud. Similarly our consciousness gets separated from our mental system. If we improve ourselves from within, then the external affairs become productive.

How We Could Control our Mental System and Mental Self?

Mental self or ego is an automatic and can be domineering if it is left unleashed. Our real self or consciousness constantly observes and control the mental self within us. Some people consider the mental self as human soul. The main problem with mental self is that mental self has no limit to its desires and has an un-satiable wants that never ends. It is our real self or consciousness that puts leash on the mental self. Our basic physical and mental needs relate to our physical and mental self, but our spiritual needs relates to our real self or consciousness. Mental self or ego has an animalistic instinct and needs and desires which relates to our basic needs such as food, water, air, sex, security, etc. and anything that is material thing. However, our real self or consciousness concentrates on our spiritual needs of transcendental and needs for getting united to the source. To suppress the un-satiable desires and constant demands of our mental self or ego, we have to have a continuous, ongoing struggle throughout our life span.

Rumi's recommendation to control the mental self is to deactivate and keep the mental system quiet. In order to deactivate the mental self, we should be able not to show any impulsive reaction to different events, incidents, situations or conditions. Because as soon as we react to any situation, our mental self becomes active and all types of racing thought processes will occur. In addition to not showing any reactions to the events, we should not travel through psychological time which is based on our mental concepts and activates our mental system. Thus we should stop our thinking process and not to think of the past or future because none of these two concepts are real, they are mental constructs. Schupp states that "thinking is stressing" and offers the technic of "not thinking" as a simple form of meditation to cope with trauma and stresses (Schupp, 2004, PP.74, 75)

Mental self is a representative of evil and evil force within the hell of mental system. Mental self not having a real base or root, tries to make self, look more authentic and strife to show that it is better and more important than what he/she really is. Our body containing both form and formlessness at the same time is presenting the existence of our physical body and etheric body or formlessness within the physical body. However, our etheric body does not have a real limit and covers inside and outside of our physical system. Life can be flowing through us and vitalize our whole system. We sleep every night and wake up in the morning based on our habits and addiction to sleep which is needed to rejuvenate us and prepare us for the next day activities. But we should also be awakened from the sleep within our mental system. The sleep within the mental system has been a very long sleep. Now it is the right time to wake up of the sleep within our mental system and stay up enough to experience the real awakening and enlightenment. When we are awakened from the sleep of the mental system, we will lose all of our pains and sufferings. Both, dreaming during the night or daydreaming during the day are perishable and fantasies that are not based on reality.

According to Rumi, if we ascend too high from the ladder of individual and group mental selves, we will fall to the ground. The more and higher we ascend, the worse our bones cracks when we fall from the artificial ladder of mental system. This ascending and descending of our mental self is very similar to the enlargement of our mental self which becomes enlarged by getting full of the empty air of grandiosity, pride and greed of un-satiated desires which turns into a balloon of air that can explode and turns into nothingness. We should be able to cancel our mental self's deficient logic and reason by preventing our mental self, from resisting and fighting with the life giving power of our universal consciousness. Stopping our mental self to get ascended or to get enlarged will help the consciousness to provide us with prosperity, joy and happiness. Acceptance of life of this moment makes it possible for the consciousness to send the divine knowledge and wisdom through us and radiate it to all other people. Consciousness within all humans can't be its own enemy and in fact it is the unifying factor among all human beings. It is mental self which search for enemy to fight with. All human beings are different forms or aspects of the same consciousness even if they come from different races, ethnicity, cultures, societies, religions or nationality.

In order to control our mental system and mental self, we should protect ourselves from the blow of intense, destructive and poisonous winds in our mental system and not to become attached and co-identified with artificial thoughts, beliefs, opinions, traditions, customs and excitement of our mental system and mental self that makes us addicted to them. One way to keep our mental self, quiet is through concentration, relaxation and meditation. We should stay away from the news that our media system try to provide us which is full of pain, sufferings, oppression, destruction, killing, genocides, some people occupying other people' land, taking over other people's life and creating hunger, misery and poverty. Most news is exaggeration of events and makes people to react negatively by creating and internalizing the pain to become more depressed or more aggressive and violent. Violence and aggression is contagious and it is negatively stimulate people, make them nervous and encourage them to create conflict and have quarrel with each other. For news people to make more money, they try to impress people more by exaggerating on the events and making it bigger than what it really is. Thus it is better not to watch the TV, listen to the Radio or read newspapers or magazines that provide us with misinformation or distorted information.

Rumi advises us to turn the sour vinegar of our mental self into the sweet syrup of consciousness by adding the sugar of joy and love until syrup of life becomes tasty and enjoyable. The biggest mistake our mental self is making is to concentrate on others and try to change them instead of working on self and change the self for the better. When we try to change others we also try to force and impose on them to accept our way of life. Rumi talks about the magic and story of "Sameri" at the base of Mount Sinai who told the Jews to bring all their golds a symbol of their attachment to this world and he made a golden cow making a cow-like sound to attract the people and to show his magical work. This was an attempt to turn the living life into a golden statue or idol. The voice of golden cow is the voice of our mental self. This happened when Moses went to Mount Sinai to bring the Ten Commandments. When Moses comes back, he became upset and showed a reaction by breaking the golden cow and putting a curse on the Sameri. This was part of Moses mental self, reacting at that moment, not his consciousness. Moses rejoined the consciousness with the experience he had at Mount Saini. However, when Jesus was betrayed by one of his disciples, he did not put curse on him, but said "Father, excuse him, because he does not know any better."

Human mental system is not only addicted to show reaction for any minor event, incident or accident but also to resist and fight back with the events or incidents. We should be aware of this addiction to events and prevent our mental self from reacting impulsively. The best way is to be patient, observe the incident, wait, analyze, comprehend and come up with the best possible solution to the problem that may emerge. We should not be afraid of incidents, try to define it as terrible or harsh and then react to the incident in a negative way. Not reacting to events, incidents or situations will help us to have enough time to review and understand what happened so that we do not make any mistakes. Our internal mate or consciousness always observes every incident and help us to make the right or the best decision regarding the incident if we be patient, wait and let our consciousness to intervene not our mental self that loves to resist and fight. The beauty and vitalizing power of mysticism will provide us with a lovely, living and exciting life. To know about the sweet taste of honey, we should taste it, to know what water can do for us we should drink it or swim in it like a fish. By talking about honey or water with a concrete concept we would never really know the nature of honey or water. A good sign of decreasing the power of our mental self is when we don't react and have the ability to apologize for our mistakes.

People who can manage their own life are above the life events and incidents and are kings of their own existence. When we engage in a positive work or activity that helps us and other people and they benefit from it, our consciousness is at work and our action is a conscious action. When we act it is our reason and life working together to help us perform an action. In order for us to jump out of the well of the mental system that we are entrapped in, we have to struggle and work hard. Being equipped with intelligence, reason and logic of living life, we have a free will and a right to choose. The more joyful we are, the more we enjoy the living life but the more we feel sad, the more we waste the living life. We should experience life as new life at any moment. To become alive we should be calm and happy. Rumi tells us that if God of love or consciousness sends the hunting dogs to catch us, we should willingly be hunted and surrender so that we can experience the sweet power of presence. If we are riding on the horse of success we should be galloping fast toward our universal consciousness and origin.

We should know that the pure consciousness only comes to human beings and penetrates within our physical and mental system because human is the representative and vehicle of the highest level of the evolution of consciousness and travel of consciousness similar to the "Ma'rhage," the ascension to the Heaven of Mohammad and his travel to the realm of unity through the universal consciousness. To go to the realm of unity, we don't need germ or physical body, only our formless weightless and germless part of our existence or consciousness can travel to the realm of unity. Rumi consider the human with developed mental self a poor and miserable being, because his/her universal consciousness is converted to physical mental consciousness within the mental self. With this experience human becomes separated from his origin and what is left is the pain of separation and anxiety, sadness, anger, fear, etc. , which is characteristics of mental self. Thus human become miserable and sorrowful. Mental self is the human unfruitful past and strives to reach to fruitfulness in the material world sometimes in the future. But real living life and fruitfulness is within us at this moment not in the outside world in the future.

At the beginning, a fetus drinks blood directly from the cord and after a child is born he/she drinks milk from mother's breast. To start the solid food a child should stop drinking milk. The same way that a fetus is imprisoned for a short while in the mother's womb, the same way human is imprisoned within the mental system and this external world for a while. Human problem is the game of chest he/she plays with consciousness. While, consciousness plays the note of joy, tranquility creativity of nothingness, the mental self plays the note of pain and sufferings of existence. The problem with existence is that it can turn to nothingness at any moment. Mental self being an artificial existence can only obtain its transitory existence within the mental system but trapped consciousness can't stay within the mental system for a long time. We are trying to checkmate the consciousness, but it is not possible, because consciousness is our real essence, we can't checkmate ourselves as consciousness.

Living in the grave of mental system is one kind of dying because the grave of mental system tries to keep us in that dark place as long as possible. But, the universal consciousness constantly works on us, and finally frees us from the dark prison and grave of mental system. The twilight of life is the distance between our mental system and nothingness. An enlightened human is the one that passes the twilight of life and enters the realm of unity and then, tries to constantly radiate the light ray of joy, tranquility and creativity toward al other beings. As human we are nailed on the cross on our four dimensions and elements of dirt, symbol of our physical body; wind, symbol of our wrong thought, beliefs and mental self; fire, a symbol of our excitements and emotions and finally; water, a symbol of our spiritual dimension. The nailing of the Christ or Messiah on the cross is a symbol of nailing the consciousness on the cross of mental system. We should not bear the pains and suffering of other individuals. Each human being should experience their own pain and suffering and become mature based on their own personal experiences. All humans will reach the treasure of presence separately not as a group or society.

Rumi uses different names for mental self, such as evil, Satan, demon, mischievous, wolf, scorpion and snake, donkey and calls mental system the hell, dark night, icy place, center of pain and suffering and burning fire. Rumi says that the lion of consciousness constantly tears our internal wolf, or the mental self, apart and finally makes us free from our internal wolves. A beautiful poem from a famous contemporary Persian poet, Fereydoon Moshiri, is in line with Rumi's ideas of considering our mental self as an internal wolf or evil which lives within us and need to be suppressed, controlled and destroyed.

"A tenacious wolf, said a wise man once, is hidden deep within each one of us.
Hence an immense daily struggle is ongoing, between the wolf and the human being.
Might alone will not this wolf subdue, one with intellect would know what to do.
Many a man, weak and grieved, have their wolves by the throat seized.
And, many a man, courageous and strong, has been trapped in their wolves' claws for long.
Whoever defeats his wolf, gradually, becomes a wholesome man, eventually. And one, who's always defeated by his wolf, may appear to be a human, but he's a wolf.
And, one with whose wolf he will conspire, wolf-like nature he will acquire.
When you're young, your wolf's life you must take,
to let him grow old with you is a grave mistake.
Even a lion of a man when he's old, is no match for a wolf who's grown old.
Whenever people tear each other apart, the wolves are their guide and steward.

Why humans are in so much pain? Because it's their wolves who have the reign.

And, tyrants who keep one another in confidence, their wolves are each other's acquaintance.

Alliance of the wolves, Estrangement of the men, of this strange state, to who may one complains? (Moshiri, Translated from Persian language to English by Franak Moshiri, 2015).

Rumi considers the bird as a symbol of consciousness and the mice as a symbol of mental self. When the bird of consciousness forget to fly or out of fear of being hunted goes into a mice hole and hide, loses its existence as a bird and lives like a mice in the dark prison of mental system. When the bird tries not to be hunted by the cats and forget about its ability to fly, then, goes into a hole and stays there. While in the mice hole, the mice forgets that once it was a bird. This is equivalent of universal consciousness which is converted to a physical and mental consciousness within the mental system and human body and forgets that once it was the universal consciousness. When the mice is involved with the food and limited place of his daily living, gradually gets adapted to that lower level style of life and forgets that a life at a higher level is possible and that as a bird it could fly freely in the sky. The mice, is not able to see the life and consciousness, thus continue to live like a form. Problem is that we use the limited and deficient reason and logic of our mental self to meet our basic needs without using our reason and logic of consciousness that is unlimited and complete. Off course we have to meet two kinds of needs, one, the worldly needs and the other one our spiritual needs. In order to reach the treasure of presence, we have to destroy the mental self. No new precious or valuable treasure can be obtained without the destruction of old place.

People who observe each other are not aware that within each form resides formlessness. Mental selves being co-identified with material and non-material things of this world introduce themselves according to their jobs such as doctor, engineer; religious figures or statuses like priest, rabbi, mullah; roles such as father, mother, daughter, brother, sister; positions such as director, manager, etc., and other forms of identifications based on status, education, religion, ethnicity, nationality, power, prestige, wealth, money, beliefs, thoughts, opinions. But we are none of these labels. These names and labels define our artificial existence just for the sake of temporary identification and are partially functional to get by in this temporary life situation, but not who we really are. Rumi says that we all commit the same sin that our first ancestors Adam and Eve committed which was, going to our mental system, developing our mental self and becoming attached, co-identified and co-dependent on the material and non-material belongings. If we desire to be accepted by the universal consciousness, then, we should repent, let go of the worldly things and get out of our evil mental system to rejoin our origin.

Rumi believes that consciousness or God possessing the power of "hearing," "seeing," and "knowing," creates a state that humans and the mental selves are being controlled through reward and punishment knowing that consciousness is constantly hearing, seeing and knowing all our behaviors. God or consciousness rules over mental selves or evil by alteration of hope and fear both are as part of our mental self's excitements. Due to human mental self or ego with excessive passions, negative thoughts, beliefs and excitement, consciousness is hearing, seeing and knowing mental selves activities at all times. Mental self does not have behavioral flexibility and is very rigid in his/her thoughts, beliefs, emotions and actions. Mental self sees everything in forms of opposites or on two extreme sides. Either something is too bad or too good, too dark or too light, too hot or too cold. The thinking pattern of mental self is dyadic, polarized and black and white. Part of the problem with mental self is that in coping with the changing social and physical environment, mental self does not have the flexibility to adapt or adjust with the rapidly changing phenomena. Mental self with a rigid interpretation of the events, situations and conditions, will distort the picture of external reality and based on wrong and distorted information makes wrong decisions and engages in wrong behaviors. Mental self, rigidity relates to his/her concrete thinking, superstitions, obsessions, stereotyping, prejudice and distorted vision.

II

Development and Establishment of Mental system and Mental Self

"It's good to leave each day behind, like flowing water, free of sadness. Yesterday is gone and its tale told. Today new seeds are growing (Rumi, 13th Cen tury)(Translated from Persian into English by: (Mafi & Kolin, 1999, P.65)

The process of the development of mental system and mental self begins right after a child is born. When the child is born his consciousness and excitements are pure, raw and neutral. Mental system starts becoming functional right after birth of a child and gradually establishes the mental self. The first child's reaction to the external world as crying and screaming occurs due to the shock he/she receives from the sudden change of environment and way of receiving oxygen from the air through his/her lung. When a child comes to this world, he/she first is given a name or a label. The child begins to know self, based on what other people call him/her. Then he becomes aware of his last name another name or concept. Later on going to school and then to the work place taking **a** variety of different positions and being assigned many roles such as daughter, son, brother, sister, father, mother, employee, director, friend, etc. takes a variety of different roles and become co-identified with those roles. Accepting many roles in society put us in a rigid framework of these roles and positions and we try to behave accordingly. However, becoming co-identified with all these roles and positions, we forget about our real objective original self.

Mental System and mental self are composed of six major subsystems or dimensions:

1. Thought, logic, reason, belief, opinion, attitudes.
2. Emotions or excitements that are considered secondary emotions such as anger, fear, and disgust
3. Feelings which are primary emotions such as worthlessness, hopelessness, helplessness, etc.
4. Social dimension or social self.
5. Individual dimension or individual self.
6. Spiritual and religious dimension.

All six dimensions are interrelated within the mental system and the established mental self within the mental system works though all these dimensions.

We are not our artificial concepts such as labels, names, roles, statuses, positions that have been assigned to us by our parents or others. Our experience is of the same substance as the matter but not consciousness. It is an event, incident or situation and condition that we should not become co-identified with. We are not our names, labels, roles, positions, traits or other adjectives that are assigned to us by others. These are only different forms of identification not our real self. The same way that child has the potential of standing on his/her feet and walking and does that with repeated trial and error until learns how to stand on his/her feet and walk as a stage in his/her physical evolution, we as adults have the potential of getting out of our mental system as a stage of evolution of our consciousness by not showing any reaction to any environmental stimuli and instead to respond correctly after we evaluate all situations thoroughly and completely.

According to Rumi, the "Mental self" arises out of interaction of each individual with his/her significant others such as our parents and relatives as well as other people around us. When a child is born, does not have a mental self. However, through people particularly parents his/her self-identity begins with the name parent use to call him/her. This name is only a mental concept and the first aspect of mental self that is being established. Immediately after this stage, the child continue internalizing information he/she receives about self from people within his/her social network and environment and gradually his/her mental self becomes more stable and rigid. Thus the way significant others and other people see the child he/she begins to become aware of him/herself as a mental self. Mental self is constantly struggling for identification and becomes co-identified with everything whether perceived as good or bad, just or unjust, as long as he/she is recognized, approved and respected by others and receives the required attention from them. Mental self becomes addicted to different labels, names, roles and has a hard time to let go of them. Because it is the nature of mental self to only add something but not to lose anything.

Freud's concept of "ego" is equivalent of Rumi's concept of "mental self" or "ego" a combination of thoughts, beliefs and excitements including our negative emotions. Freud's concept of "super-ego," is considered equivalent of Rumi's "real, objective or original consciousness," an ever knowing, selfless, formless, eternal and unlimited consciousness. Rumi believes that the "mental self" is the main cause of all psychological, emotional, mental and physical pains, while the "real, objective or original self," is the cause of our joy, happiness, tranquility and creativity. Rumi's idea of consciousness is equivalent of Freud's "Super ego." According to Rumi, our consciousness as an extension of universal consciousness does not have a physical body. It is formless, timeless, limitless, eternal and nothing within everything. If we try to search for anything but our universal consciousness, we are bound to be attached to them including the material objects and things of the external world.

Rumi believes that we as human being who live with other people are constantly under influence of the family, group or society. We become aware of ourselves and our personality through the eyes of other people, thus our mental self which is composed of both individual self and social self are not really different from each other, but we act differently when we are alone and when we are in group, because within the group many eyes are looking and observing us and they can influence and control our behaviors at all times. Rumi's concept of "mental self," corresponds to James's concept of material self. His concept of "social mental self," is equivalent to James's social self, and his concept of real, objective, original self is parallel to James's spiritual self. According to James, the individual has as many social selves as there are distinct groups and collectivity of attitudes. He offered three types of selves. (1) Material self, consist of things that belong to us or that we belong to things such as our family, our body, and money.(2) Social self, who we are in a given situation, and (3) spiritual self, who are at our core. The spiritual self is more concrete than the other two selves. James's theory of self is divided into two related parts, the "me" and the "I" (James, 1890).

While Rumi talks about the community of attitudes, beliefs, thoughts, opinions that an individual internalizes through mutual interaction and becomes aware of his/her mental self, Mead also believed that self, arises out of interaction of the individual with both "significant others" and "generalized others." In line with James, Mead elaborated on two separate parts of the self the "I" and the "Me". Mead, developed the Concept of self, however, divided the "self" into two parts, the "I" and the "Me". The "I" and the "Me" is not the same, they are two stages and sub-units of the self. The "Me", is the internalized attitudes of others about self and the "I" is the response of the self to the attitudes of others. According to Mead, the self, arises in the process of social interaction and activity (Mead, 1934) . To Rumi consciousness is our mirror and our body is the dirt and rust that covers the face of the mirror. The consciousness or "truth," is our "real self" hidden within our Phenomenal and visible self or physical body.

Rumi distinguishes between the mental self and the real, objective self. 1. The mental self is an artificial, distorted and false sense of self which has physical and mental consciousness similar to plants and animals and can be only aware of other forms, his belongings and thought, belief and excitement. Mental self, desires to have a sense of identification, security and happiness, but all his desires are psychological in nature and distorted not based on real needs. Mental self is only a reflection and picture of real self. But, the real, objective self which has consciousness of presence and experiences the living life does not need artificial psychological needs, because it is formless, timeless and eternal. Consciousness of presence consciously observes everything as formless consciousness not material forms. The real self is formless, objective, unlimited, eternal, complete, creative, peaceful, independent and joyful and works with love, tranquility, creativity, and productivity. However, the mental self is a form, picture, reflection, temporary, deficient, transitory, blind, co-identified, attached, and co-dependent and works with thought, belief, opinion, custom, rite, and excitement and likes to resist, fight and destroy everybody and everything.

We should be aware of the major limitation of our mental system to learn about the self, society and the universe and comprehend the complicated nature of our life. Our mental self has to play with concepts in our mental system to create artificial concepts that are match with things that are external to self. However, our mental system is limited by duality, comparison, classification, generalization, deletion, registration, and storing information. Our mental system only work with time and is also limited by our verbal and written language which every act has to be identified in the past, present or the future. Our mental system thus, is limited to comprehend only the parts as separated phenomena and is not able to observe or understand the whole or the unity. Mental self does not have life of its own. It is only a reflection of the real self and life. All the enjoyment of mental physical self is temporary and transitory. The enjoyment is very short lived and will soon ends. Rumi says that mental self's enjoyment of material things in this world is very similar to a sweet pastry which is only sweet for a short time when it is in our mouth. As soon as we swallow the pastry, the sweet taste is gone.

Rumi believed that mental self or ego is established through interaction of an individual with his/her parents and others and becomes aware of his/her mental self through the reaction or response of people around him/her. Cooley's conception of the "self" corresponds to William James's social self and Rumi's mental self. Cooley calls it "Looking glass–self". According to Cooley, "the self, arises dialectically through communication. Cooley tried to show the reflective characteristic of self by comparing it to a looking glass-self" (Cooley, 1930). It has been thousands of years that human has been imprisoned within the forms and finally within the human mental system. Searching for the truth within the mental system with its major limitation regarding time, location, space, thought, beliefs, opinions, excitements our mental self does not have the ability to comprehend the universal consciousness or reality of our origin. Mental self has a material idol outside self and reduces the universal consciousness to persons, objects, idol and statue within the external world not being aware that the extension of universal consciousness is within itself.

According to Rumi, if we do not become aware of our real, objective, original self, we will remain in the dark prison of our mental system for the rest of our life. Our mental system, is the prison, and the center of our evilness, pains and the internal hell, where we constantly debating and discriminating and trying to make a choice between the evil metal self and the transcendental real, objective or original self. We have to resolve the major internal conflict which, exists within us before we can reach to the real tranquility, and joy of life. While the mental self is using the mental system including our thoughts, beliefs, excitements to relate to the external world, the real, objective, original self as an extension of total and absolute consciousness works through love to bring us joy and happiness. Rumi believes that love is the major cement and motivational power of the universe and works within all parts of the universe and through this unity holds everything together. Love is our awakening from the deep sleep of mental system and its agent mental self and to become one with our origin or universal consciousness.

We are able to see our physical self through a mirror, however, seeing and observing our mental self is more important even if we are not able to see our mental self. To see and observe our mental self, we need to let our real objective self or consciousness to observe and be aware of our mental self through the concentration and observation of our thought, belief, opinion, excitement and action. Of course our action is highly dependent on the way we think, feel and analyze our situation at any moment. When we evaluate ourselves we become aware of our mental self. However, our mental self is constantly changing based on our new experiences. If we change our definition of ourselves, then, we can change our self-concept. When we modify the definition of ourselves, we will have a new concept of self whether it is the mental self or physical self. Similarly when we have any type of surgery, and change our physical appearance, we would have a new definition of our physical self. Our awareness of our physical and mental self comes from our experience regarding our physical self and from how other people react toward us regarding our mental self. We should construct a correct self-concept based on our real traits.

Human knowledge is based on the self-experience in the past and, experiences of all other human before him/her. It is based on human mental system and active mental self with all the thoughts, beliefs, excitements and emotions. Anything that passes through our mental system is considered mental experience. The experiencer precedes the experience itself. There would not be any experience without a being to experience. Sensual activities and processes are also experience. To have a dream we have to have a dreamer. Human experience is being completed through three of our major dimensions. 1. Human five major senses that are based on our nervous system and are our most basic vehicle or connection to our external world, 2. Human excitements or emotions, such as: fear, anger, rage, jealousy, greed, and, 3. Human mental system and the related thought, belief, opinions. Some people think that if we improve our external life we will become happy internally. But this is only a delusion. Happiness comes from inside of human consciousness not from outside world. If we are happy inside we can be happy no matter where we go and if we are sad and unhappy, it does not make any difference where we are.

Attachment, Co-identification and Codependency: A Natural Tendency of Mental Self

We use our perception to give material objects and things a sense of identification and then become co-identified by those material objects. With our physical mental self-consciousness at each moment we become aware of a thoughts, beliefs, opinions, excitements, events or material objects. However, these thoughts, beliefs, opinions, excitements, events or material objects are in constant state of change. Thus, we should not to become co-identified with any of these different aspects of our mental self or any events for a long time and should not show any reaction to them. Using our mental system is functional for a temporary time until we receive enough experience from the external world. Another aspect of our mental self is to experience dreams, however, these dreams are nightmares associated with distortions, pain and suffering. These nightmares occur in our mental system during the day. However, we also experience dreams in our sleep. In order to dream there has to be a dreamer which is our real, objective, original and spiritual self.

When mental self is established in human mental system, it temporarily goes to sleep in the mental system and becomes separated and disconnected from the universal consciousness. Due to separation from the source, mental self, suffers with variety of emotional, psychological, mental and physical pain which include the major sense of deficiency. In order to reduce the deficiency, mental self goes after external forms and becomes co-identified and attached with the material things. Mental self tries to make self, more important by attaching roles, positions, social status, power, prestige, and material belongings to itself and create a new sense of ownership of all types of things including the members of his/her family. However, adding and owning all these perishable items is a temporary satisfaction and does not last long. Having or owning all the possible material belongings can't satisfy the main value of "to be," or "to become," or "to do." As a result of this form of co-identification and attachment with worldly things, mental self loses its independence completely and search for more co-identification and attachment, thus, mental self tries to attach itself to the group and the power and energy of the group and identify self as "we", a new group co-identification.

Rumi tells a story in a poem form about a snake-catcher who would amuse people with snakes and was making money that way. He found a huge snake (python) in the mountain which was frozen by the cold and in a deep sleep, and imagining it to be dead, he tied it up and took it to Baghdad in Iraq, on the bank of Euphrates River. He was bragging and showing off that he was able to kill such a huge snake. Gradually as the weather became warmer, the snake thawed by the warmth of the sun, recovered life and began swallowing the spectators, curling itself around a tree and breaking their bones and killing them. The dead snake is a symbol of worldly things that we get attached to or become co-identified with similar to other important worldly materials such as money, wealth, luxury, etc. which distract us in life and swallow us at any moment. The spectators were the symbol of mental selves that were fascinated by the snake and the snake handler amusement of daily life and distractions from life. Thus, to become co-identified with the worldly stuff is a mistake and is considered a sin because it only causes pain for us. As we drop one of the material or non-material object or thought of this world, we are being pulled upward toward the realm of unity.

Rumi's idea about mental self's characteristics as hate, vengefulness and conflict as well as attachment, codependency and co-identification with material things and passions are in line with Buddha's concepts of "dvesha" or avoidance and hatred and "avida" or ignorance (Wikipedia, the Free Encyclopedia) which is related to human over-dependency and attachment to material life, passion and basic physical, social needs. It is the essence and nature of mental system and mental self to get attached to thoughts, beliefs, opinions, excitements and material objects of this world. All our thoughts, beliefs, opinions, excitements, roles, positions, power, privilege, social status and material belongings, even our physical body and mental system and its agent mental self are temporary, transitory and perishable, thus attaching to perishable things is a bad sign that we are made of perishable items. However, our universal consciousness is eternal, unlimited, timeless and formless. Thus, we should become aware of our origin and become one with it. The major responsibility of mental self within our mental system is to work with duality of life the only way we can make sense of external reality. Without thinking about duality and comparing two opposites, our mental system becomes paralyzed and we can't relate to external world. However, when mental self considers everything as opposite to every other thing a major conflict will be created in life.

Mental self is deficient and tries to make self, look complete by engaging in lies and deception to put self under positive light. When mental self suddenly reacts to another person's mental self it is because mental self, see some negative trait in another person which his/herself possess. Rumi sees mental self's action as putting our hands in a snake den and being bitten by the snake. He believes that our negative thoughts, beliefs, excitements and that of others are like snake bites that we constantly experience. In order not to get bitten, it is better to stay away from these types of wrong excitements. Our universal consciousness tries to keep us away from snake bites but our mental self never listens or pay any attention. Our universal consciousness tries to help us to change our "to be," into "to become" and "to do." Being dissatisfied with our daily living which is the major characteristic of our mental self, we always think that we do not have enough money, material things, power, education, position and other worldly things. This is because our mental self is measuring life with the ruler of mental system which is not accurate.

To show the limitation of the knowledge of mental self, and limitation of our knowledge based on the study of separated or scattered parts of a phenomenon and then, engaging in a wrong generalization from one small part to the whole system, Rumi talks about a story of an elephant in a dark room. Several people went to a dark room and touched different parts of an elephant and each provided the result of their experience. One touched the elephant's ear and said it was a large fan. The second person touched a leg of elephant and said it was a pillar. The third person touched the elephant's back and said it was a great thorn. The fourth person touched the elephant's nose and said it was a water pipe. Their generalization from one body part of the elephant to what they thought as the whole system was wrong. What those people used as devices of examining the elephant was their sense and biased mental judgement that was insufficient to know the reality of the phenomenon. All of their information and judgements was wrong. All they needed was to have a light to see and use all their devices and senses to comprehend the elephant in its entirety. We have the same problem in our mental system which is limited in knowledge. We need our universal consciousness to light up our horizon and help us to understand all the phenomena.

Rumi recommends that we should go back and forth between the mental system the center of duality and the realm of unity and oneness to bring the joy, happiness and creativity of the realm of unity to our daily life. Any time mental self tries to cause pain and suffering we should use our consciousness to eliminate the sadness and depression of our mental self. We should remind our self that we are not form, water, dirt, wind, fire, body, mental system, senses, thought, excitement or pain but a living life of consciousness. We are hearing the drums of conversion of our physical and mental consciousness to the universal consciousness. Thus, we should be prepared for a trip from this world and our mental system to the realm of unity. The external world is pregnant with the world of unity and is going to give birth to a new world of presence and unity. Thus, Maryam is pregnant with Messiah, our Godly origin and consciousness. This is the natural process of evolution of consciousness.

Reactive Nature of Mental Self

Reactivity particularly impulsive reaction to the neutral events, incidents, situations and conditions is nearly the main source of all our problems. Mental self is highly reactive to any event, incident, situation or condition. In fact mental self makes self, more important and rigid by engaging in reactivity toward anything that happens around him/her in the immediate social and physical environment. Due to suspiciousness, lack of trust and paranoia that mental self, experiences, and a tendency to exaggerate, he/she shows an intense negative reaction toward any event or incident. Mental self takes any event as an excuse to react to. If someone is looking at a person with rigid mental self, he/she may object to the other person and ask him/her why he/she is being looked at. If someone is saying something neutral, a person with rigid mental self, will personalize it and show negative reaction by negatively perceiving the other person's speech. Reactive tendency of mental self creates various problems in its social relationships with others. Whatever happens around a person with mental rigidity, the mental self has to say something about it, because mental self is highly active with racing thought process and negative excitements and loves to talk constantly to relieve the obsessive thoughts and reach to a level of compulsion.

Rumi talks about a story in Koran about prophets Moses and Khizr who is symbol of consciousness and eternal life which was found of calmness and wisdom. Rumi uses this story to show negative consequences of reactivity. Moses before reaching to the treasure of presence and deactivating his mental system was accompanying Khizr in a trip. Moses showed several reactions and asked a lot of questions as related to different events that occurred during their trip. Khizr offers Moses a condition and rule of conduct that he should stay quiet, deactivate his mental system and not to ask many questions. Mental hyperactivity and asking many questions is the characteristic of mental self. Khizr and Moses walked together and traveled together. On their way they came upon a wall that was disintegrating. Khizr repaired the wall for someone without asking for any money. Moses tells Khizr why you did not charge the person for the repair of the wall. He reminds Moses of the condition of being quiet and tells Moses that when you are with me you should be blind and deaf and quiet.

Continuing their trip, on the way Khizr kills a young man (Symbolically means killing an evil mental self) who was a symbol of a dangerous mental self and Moses complains and criticizes Khizr. He reminds Moses again about the agreement they had. While travelling on a boat, Khizr notices a few boats are getting near them and immediately makes a hole in the boat. Moses again complains and Khizr tells him that he was prejudging constantly. Finally Khizr explain to Moses that the reason I did not charge any money for the wall was that there was a treasure inside the wall and the thieves could take that money. The reason I killed the young man was that he was a symbol of a dangerous mental self and an artificial mental self must be destroyed.

Then, he explains that the reason that I made a hole in the boat was to prevent the great mental self or king and his people from taking and occupying our boat. Thus any event or incident that may look bad to us may turn to be the best event. The boat here is a symbol of our mental system that needed to be destroyed. The young man was the symbol of a mental self who could destroy innocent people. The wall is the symbol of the boundary between the mental self and the consciousness or the treasure of presence.

Mental self is very impatient and does not want to wait for anything. Being impatient, the mental self, acts very impulsive without giving it any deep thought. Mental self does not plan ahead for anything he/she is going to obtain, thus, tries to gain whatever he/she desires right away. Rumi uses a story of the porky pine hunting the snake to show that how reacting impulsively to the events, incidents and situations can be destructive. Porky pine grabs snake by the tail and wait patiently. The snake being in a hurry to escape, hits its body to the body of porky pine which is full of sharp blades, over and over again, and loses enough blood to get killed and then, porky pine eats the snake without any struggle. If the snake would not react impulsively and could be patient, there was possibility that the porky pine would get tired and let go of the snake. Thus the impulsive reaction of the snake brings the snake to its death. Similar to Rumi's emphasis on reaction being the main cause of mental self's various problems in his/her daily life, Eysenck (1959) believed that abnormal behaviors are learned pathological behavior reaction to simple neutral stimuli. There are no obscure "causes" which "underlie" pathological behavior reactions, there is merely the reaction itself; modify the reaction, or the conditions which precipitate it, and you have eliminated all there is to pathology (in, Millon & Millon, 1974, P. 189).

In order to be happy, joyful and creative, we should let our consciousness to work through us not our mental self which causes nothing but pain of negative thoughts, beliefs, and excitements. If we react to different situations, conditions, events or incidents, it means that our mental self is active and causing problems. Thus, by not impulsively reacting to our environmental events and incidents, we make our mental self, inactive and keep our mental system quiet. The more we keep our mental system quiet and reduce the compulsive mental thinking that bothers us like the constant sounds of bees, the more creative thinking, joy and tranquility of the mind of our consciousness we experience. Rumi distinguishes between the vine of life and the grape vine. Both makes us drunk but while the grape vine makes us drunk and unaware of the external reality which is crippling process of our mind, the vine of life makes us high, joyful and creative and sharpens our mind. The vine of life comes from our universal consciousness which resides within all creatures of the universe and everything and we should be aware of ourselves as consciousness not the physical body and mental system.

III

Evolution of Consciousness and Temporary Mental Self within the Mental System

*"The Evolution of Man - First he appeared in the class of
inorganic things, next he passed there from into that of plants.
For years he lived as one of the plants, remembering naught of
his inorganic state so different; and when he passed from the
vegetative to the animal state. He had no remembrance of his
state as a plant... drew man out of the animal into the human
state. Thus man passed from one order of nature to another, till
he became wise and knowing and strong as he is now. Of his first
soul he has now remembrance, and he will be again changed from
his present soul. In order to escape from his present soul full of lusts
he must behold thousands of reasonable souls. Though man fell
asleep and forgot his previous states, yet God will not leave him
in this self-forgetfulness, and then he will laugh at his own former
state, Saying, "What mattered my experiences when asleep? When
I had forgotten my prosperous condition, and knew not that the
grief and ills I experienced were the effect of asleep and illusion
and fantasy? ..." (Rumi, 13ᵗʰ Century) (Translated from Persian
language into English by: E. H. Whinfield, PP. 148, 149).*

Rumi asks himself and all humans: who are we and who do we look like?
He then, answers: We don't look like anything or anybody. We are made of
consciousness and godliness, the formlessness, timelessness, unlimited, and

eternal. We have our own essence and originality free of forms, roles, physical, mental or anything of this world. At one moment I look like an angel made of beauty, tranquility and creativity and in another moment I sing the song and note of the angel. We are free like the wind at one moment and trapped in the form in another moment but that does not change our essence. We are not form and we should not be attached or co-identified with other forms. Even after, we go, into the forms of solids, plants, animals and human and get temporarily trapped in those forms we stay there temporarily. When we reach to human and resides in human mental system, it is to experience the world and evolve to a higher level of consciousness so that we can rejoin the universal consciousness.

Rumi's (13th Century, around 1240s) definition of consciousness is "energy, light and force" that exist within all the particles of the universe. According to him, the universal consciousness has migrated from solids to the plants, from plants to the animals and from animals to the human. While in human, consciousness is trapped and stays within human physical and mental system and finally it will release itself and rejoin the universal consciousness. To Rumi the universal consciousness is the essence of all things and creatures. It is formless, timeless, limitless and eternal. Thus, consciousness is considered by Rumi as a universal phenomenon. However, other people defined consciousness as awareness, alertness, knowing, and knowledge characteristics of human mind. Wallace and Fisher (1987, 1983) summarized some of the definitions of the consciousness from Oxford English Dictionary and James. "Consciousness as the function of knowing" (James, 1890, 1904); "Joint or mutual knowledge, "Internal knowledge or conviction" "State of awareness," "Direct awareness," (Natsoulas, 1978a); "Personal unity," (Natsoulas, 1978a 1978b; Oxford English Dictionary); "Personal unity," (Oxford English Dictionary; "Multi states of information processing or double consciousness" (Natsoulas, 1978a, 1978b)" (Wallace & Fisher, 1987, 1983, PP.3-5). All these definitions relate to human knowing, knowledge and the degree of awareness and alertness. Rumi's definition of consciousness given approximately 800 years ago before all these individuals, include all these characteristics and include God or consciousness as energy and light with all the possible knowledge, knowing, awareness, alertness and the universal unity.

Rumi reminds us that even before the emergence of human being on this planet, the universal consciousness was in the process of evolution through solids, plants, and animals. When consciousness tried to evolve at a higher level in human it penetrated human physical and mental system. Through physical system, human became able to experience the external world through senses and the nervous system and through our mental system consciousness began to take the form of mental consciousness using our brain and mind, thought, beliefs, opinions and excitements to mentally experience the external reality. Thus the universal consciousness did not only penetrated into the physical system of the special people such as prophets, mystics, saints, and those who reached the treasure of presence, but also penetrated within the physical and mental system of all human species. The only difference between the special people and other people is that the special people reached a higher level of consciousness through concentration, meditation, relaxation and comprehension of their real essence but other people are still trapped within their mental system. Now, we all need to do the same and try to free ourselves out of our mental system and rejoin our origin which is the universal consciousness.

According to Rumi, after mental self is established within the mental system through the interaction of a child with his/her immediate social and physical environment gradually it reaches to a sense of existence and becomes hardened and rigid through time. The more a child internalizes the ideas, attitudes, thought and beliefs of other people around him, the more rigid his/her mental self becomes. As the social circles of the child grows and he/she ages, and interacts with more people and becomes more experienced, he/she becomes more aware of his/her mental self. However, the process of the evolution of consciousness within the child's mental system and mental self occurs parallel to the larger scale evolution of consciousness in the universe which is automatic and that mental self can't stop this process of evolution. The evolution of consciousness and all forms are from the matter toward pure universal consciousness. Thus all forms and anything in this known universe is temporary and perishable. Nothing is permanent except the universal consciousness which is timeless, formless, eternal, and unlimited.

To Rumi, the whole world and its constituent parts are in a constant state of evolution and change. The universal consciousness is penetrating into forms and travels from one form to another form and changes from one state to another newer state. However, this evolution is from lower degree to a higher degree of consciousness. Always with a right and timely move of the consciousness from a lower level to a higher one, consciousness will continue to evolve where it is most effective. Thus going through the solids, plants, animals, finally consciousness goes into the human and human mental system and begins to evolve and change the mental self. However, like every other worldly thing, human mental self has to help the physical consciousness to become mature and jump out of the mental system to become selfless and part of universal consciousness. Before the emergence of human being the direction of the evolution of consciousness was from universal consciousness toward human beings through solids, plants and animals until it reach the human. But after the emergence of human species, the direction of the evolution of consciousness is from human mental system toward the universal consciousness. Thus the direction of evolution of consciousness is upward from solid, through plants and animals to human being and through spiritual and transcendental growth back to the universal consciousness. Our human consciousness can't go back to previous forms such as animals or plants.

Rumi believes that the whole world with all planets, stars, suns, and other germs and all phenomena, things and creatures are dancing and moving toward a pre-destined direction. Life is nothing but the continuous non-stop dance of the forms which vibrate according to the universal pulse of the consciousness. But becoming prisoner of the mental system and letting our mental self to decide and take action we do not achieve anything but pain. Mental self gets attached to worldly things and with each attachment creates a new form of co-identification which is painful. However, all types of pain such as physical, mental, psychological and spiritual pain and sufferings are awakening and provide us with an awareness that something is really wrong and we should not stay within the mental system for a long time. While animals are instinctually joyful and playful, human using the mental system becomes sad and unhappy because of all the negative thoughts, beliefs and excitement.

Human is the last frontier of the evolution of consciousness which jumps out of our mental system and will be converted from the physical and mental consciousness to the universal consciousness. Each human has the history of the evolution of consciousness and all the life experiences of all the human generations within him/her and transfer part of the consciousness to the next generations of human beings. Consciousness tries to become alive in human. Consciousness created the whole universe as forms to experience itself within the forms. All forms change to other new forms or dissolves at the final stage, but consciousness is eternal and never dies. The major difference between human being and life forms before human is that solids had consciousness of the solids, plants have consciousness of vegetation, animals have consciousness and instinct but their consciousness is at the level of animal consciousness. Human, while having instincts, has the ability to suppress or control part of the animalistic instinct, but is the main and final vehicle of the evolution of consciousness. It is in human that consciousness reaches to its highest level of transcending, where is able to rejoin the universal consciousness.

According to Rumi, there are four main stages of the evolution of consciousness within human beings. Universal consciousness is extended within human physical and mental dimensions. Stage1, Include the penetration of the universal consciousness into fetus in the mother's womb. Stage 2, Include the penetration of the consciousness into the child's mental system right after he/she is born, Stage 3, Include obtaining experience and reaching to a maturity level within and through the mental system, and Stage 4, Completes the process of the freedom of consciousness from the temporary prison of mental system and rejoining the universal consciousness. All creatures in the universe represent different forms of consciousness in different stages of evolution.

Even plants and animals represent different forms of consciousness. We don't need to struggle to reach to the transcendental consciousness we already have it within us as humans. All we need is to become aware of it and recognize it. In order to be able to become aware of our universal transcendental consciousness is to keep our mental system quiet. We can experience consciousness in two forms: 1. through, our mental self as a mental consciousness, and 2. through a complete experience of unity and oneness with consciousness.

Rumi identified two main stages of human life as consciousness. The first stage is to gain experience through the major senses, nervous system, mental operation of receiving the environmental stimuli and data, analyzing the data, classifying the information, generalizing the data, registering the data, storing or deleting the data and finally making a decision and taking action. We should be aware that our mental system and mental self has physical mental consciousness which works based on a linear time and consciousness, thus, it is very limited to time and the events of the past, present and future. In fact it is our consciousness which is experiencing the external world through our physical mental system. The second stage is for our physical mental consciousness to jump out of our mental system to be free from the bondage of physical, mental consciousness and rejoin the universal consciousness. When Consciousness penetrates into human body creates its identical state in two types of consciousness. One is physical consciousness that resides within the whole physical system, and the other one is mental consciousness within the mental system.

To achieve the first purpose in our life, we need to accept the external reality as it is without any resistance and judgement and live parallel to the normal natural human life. To achieve the second purpose, we should try to identify our deficiencies, short comings and wrong habits of co-identification with the external world and one by one to cut the cord of co-identification and attachment to the worldly phenomena such as material belongings, our roles as father, mother, brother, sister, son, daughter, friends, relatives, our thought belief, opinion and excitements. This will help us gradually to get rid of our attachments one by one. The more we throw away and cut the cords of our attachments, the closer we get to the universal consciousness. Rumi believes that, universal consciousness constantly and gradually helps us to get out of the prison of mental system and pulls the physical mental consciousness over itself. Our internal consciousness is aware of all the thoughts, beliefs, opinions, excitements and activities we engage throughout our life span. Everything we think, we say, or we do will be registered and stored within our mental system. Any time our consciousness decides to review what we have done, it can open and read our life history within our mental system like a book.

Consciousness, have been considered as light and energy by most people and all ceremonies and parties of people are associated with light. Persian New year, "Noroos" means new day which is celebrated on the first day of spring and is associated with light, brightness and revitalization of life. Zoroastrian had a very high respect for fire and light and would keep fire and candles lighted in their temples at all times. Moslem's celebration of "Eid-al-Fitr," the festival of fast breaking, celebration with family and friends and the completion of a month of blessing and joy is related to the change in the state of the moon light, brightness and purification of body and soul, abstinence, acceptance and surrendering to God or consciousness. Jewish "Hanukah" also is associated with light and brightness. Their candle holder with eight lights of candles is symbol of light and brightness. The Christmas' celebration of "Easter" Jesus birth day is also associated with the birth of consciousness and light.

The Chinese New year originally tied to the lunar-solar calendar (Random House Dictionary, 2016). The light system of energy or universal consciousness is the common denominator of all the particles of the universe. Under certain pressure and temperature any material or substance in the universe can turn into flame, fire and light. This is because the light system of energy and consciousness resides within every particles of the universe. In fact the origin of the whole universe is started by an explosion of the light system of energy. The theory of "Big bang" is a good example of this idea. Almost all members of different religious and none religious people no matter what type of religion they have respect the light and brightness. Lighting up candles in the mosques, churches, and synagogues, and different temples or places of worships is very common practice.

According to Rumi, consciousness within human body is divided into two types of consciousness. One is the mental consciousness which becomes trapped within our mental system and creates our mental self and the other one is the physical consciousness which resides within the whole human body. Rumi compare the consciousness and human body with a clipper. The static arm of the clipper is considered consciousness and the moving arm of the clipper which moves in a circle is the human. To get farther from the stationary arm the moving arm makes bigger circle but it would be away from the stationary arm. Moslems who circle around the Kaaba move around it in circle. But what we really need to do is to circle around the life of this moment within us which is consciousness. The life of this moment is the stationary arm of the clipper and the center of the circle and as humans we should circle around ourselves like the moving arm of the clipper.

The world and mental self is like a snake that is coiling and sleeping over a treasure. The treasure is the realm of unity and the snake of mental self is over it and spreads the pain everywhere. The emerald or consciousness makes the eyes of the snake of mental self, blind.

We should not beg or bend over to any external object including building or metallic, golden, silver objects to help us or give us a favor or change our life for the better, we should look inside ourselves for help where our living consciousness is resided. Consciousness is penetrated in us as empty space and resides within every particle of our every cell and as science explains within each cell we have atoms and within each atom we have electron, neutron, proton and the nuclei. The electrons are dancing and revolving around the nuclei. The smallest parts of cells are quarks. Within the quarks there is space full of energy. Even within and between the electron, neutron and proton there is empty space full of energy. This type of space is within everything and any parts of the universe. The empty spaces which are full of energy contain consciousness which is calm, relaxed and quiet. The empty space exists both within and without us. We as unlimited and eternal consciousness can't stay within our mental system which can comprehend the world either with psychological time or with six positional directions such as the east, west, north, south, up and down. The space that includes all the solar systems, suns, moons, etc. is more important than all the solar germs, because without the unlimited space these germs could not reside.

Rumi uses an analogy between the water and consciousness. He says the same way that water is trapped in the dirt and mud is made, the same way consciousness will be trapped in the form including human body and mental system. Water tries to evaporate from the mud, but mud grabs the water hard and does not let go of the water, because if water leaves the only thing that remains is dirt. The same way our physical body and mental system does not let go of trapped consciousness, because when the consciousness is gone, what remains is a dead physical and mental body. Mud is jealous of water that is flowing into and over everything. If mud loses its water, it become solid dirt and has to stay where it is. The same way human body and mental system is jealous of consciousness and does not let go of it. Consciousness desires to leave our body but we help our physical mental system to hold the consciousness through resistance and fighting. Mental system pulls us toward the transitory material world but our consciousness pulls us toward eternal, spiritual world.

As we grow older the level of energy decreases and tells us that the migration of our life consciousness out of our physical and mental system is near. Our joy, activity level and movement decreases and we realize that our physical body and mental self is only temporary and our consciousness which is eternal and unlimited formless and timeless always exist as nothingness. When the light of consciousness passes through us, we feel a sense of unity, joy and tenderness. Our loneliness and sadness goes away. But our mental self is very persistent in resisting and tries to maintain the pains and sufferings. If we observe our mental self and stop it from deviant thought and action, we can be effective in transferring knowledge and peacefulness to other people. Rumi also uses the word "Dajjal" as representative of evil which spreads a carpet of fire to burn everybody, but Messiah destroy the antichrist and imposter of excitement, sorrow and pain with his sword of consciousness.

IV

Functions of Mental System and Mental Self (Ego)

Positive Functions of Mental Self and Mental System

God is the author of good and evil. Evil itself is turned into good for the good (Rumi,13ᵗʰ Century) Translated from Persian into English Language by: Whinfield (1898, PP. 65, 66)

Mental system is a necessary and complementary part of our existence but it is a temporary device to provide us with life experiences and bring us to the point of maturity. We receive our data and information through our senses, then, our mental system using the brain analyze, compare, classify and generalize, retrieve and store, register the useful information in our mind and delete the repetitive unnecessary information. Through this type of activity we make a sense of external reality which includes the social and physical environmental aspects of our life. Based on the information we receive and process, then, we make decision and act accordingly. However if we establish a rigid mental self and become co-identified and co-dependent with different aspects of our life situations, conditions, and incidents as well as our material belongings, our thoughts, beliefs and opinions within our social and physical environment, then we will create all kinds of problems and pains for ourselves.

Some of the mental system and mental self, processes could have positive and/or negative functions. Two of Rumi's poems entitled "God the Author of Good and Evil," and "Evil itself is turned into good for the good," tries to show the positive function of mental system and mental self or evil. To organize the knowledge and information the function of generalization and comparison is positive. However, when we use generalization to generalize a negative trait from one person to the group or when we compare self with others and try to show that we are better than them the function becomes negative. By using our mental system we develop our mental self which is functional for us to relate to our social and physical environment and consequently receive enough knowledge and information through different media system, schooling, studies, books, internet, etc. we do not really need our highly established mental self that causes all kinds of psychological, mental, emotional, and physical pain for us forever. Instead what we need is our real self that is parallel and in line with our real life without resistance, conflict, fighting, anger, aggression, rage, fear, greed, jealousy, blaming others, expecting others to do things for us, putting other people down, sadness and many other negative characteristics of mental self. Partial evil of mental self appears opposed to unity or consciousness because mental self with mental and physical consciousness is not able to comprehend consciousness through the limited knowledge of mental system, but serves a positive function unconsciously.

The wind during the spring and in a spring-like climate or environment has the positive function of rejuvenating life of plants, flowers and everything in the nature and makes all human being joyful and relaxed, however, the same wind during the fall and within the cold weather and climate, makes trees to lose their leaves and flowers to perish and makes human sad and sick. The difference between the positive power of the wind and the negative power of the wind is considerable, one being constructive and the other one being destructive. There is also a main difference between the climate of unity and universal consciousness which provides us with joy, happiness, relaxation and tranquility and the fall of mental system which provides us with negative thought, beliefs, and excitement which includes sadness and depressed mood. In order for our total consciousness to be more functional and let it work through us and lead us using the real knowledge and wisdom, our mental self should be calm and quiet and stop the racing thought process and the buzzing sound of the bee inside our mental system. Within our mental system, the mental self with different addictive traits is controlling our life and does not let us to be free.

In order to show the positive function of mental self and creating excessive pain within the mental system, so that our trapped consciousness could jump out of our mental system, Rumi provides a beautiful story of a Lady cooking chickpeas in the pan over the stove. Due to the heat and getting tortured in the hot water, chickpeas peas were trying to cope with the situation by jumping up and down in the water experiencing the dance of getting mature and cooked. The chickpeas constantly were complaining and trying to escape the heat and fire trying to come up to the surface of the water in the pan, but the lady would hit them on the head to push them down the pan and mix them to let every one of them to have equal chance of getting cooked. The lady tells the chickpeas that I am trying to make you tasty by adding spices and make you edible, because you become part of the life of human beings. What you lose is your rawness and what you gain is maturity, functionality and usefulness. Thus, the pain and suffering you experience is the test of your ability to become functional and productive. It is the grand plan of life to extract the consciousness from a sense of existence and forms.

The lady in this story is considered as a symbol of God or consciousness. Split peas are symbols of raw humans mental selves who need to be matured, cooked and suffer the pain of hell fire within the mental system. The pan is a symbol of the space within the mental system, and the fire under the Pan is the symbol of the pains of mental selves. Like split peas which were jumping up and down complaining the pain from the heat and fire, mental selves constantly complain about the pains within the mental system. People say oh God you have created us then, why we should go through all these pains and suffering. God will tell humans that you need to boil, find out about your deficiencies, get cooked and mature, and pains forces you to jump up and down but the main function of all these pain and sufferings is to make you become aware of your own miseries within the mental system so that you would willingly and voluntarily accept and surrender to the universal consciousness and free yourself from the prison of mental self and all the attachments and co-identifications.

Negative Functions of Mental System and Mental Self (Ego) and Mental System: A Source of Negative Excitement, Emotion and sadness

According to Rumi, the mental system and the corresponding mental self has the major function of creating so much pain that causes us to jump out of the prison of mental system and suppress our mental self that kept us separate from our source and origin the universal consciousness. Mental self is created within our mental system when mental self develops a sense of existence and identification and consider self as real which is not the case, because the mental self is an artificial, quasi and temporary reflection of our real self. However, with the help of our mental system which brings us to the point of giving up our mental self, the universal consciousness will rejoins and absorbs our mental and physical consciousness to self. Then, the major goal of all human beings is to obtain enough experience through their mental system and senses and through love to become one with their origin and life which is universal consciousness. Rumi believes that all human are connected to the universal consciousness at all times, but our mental system and mental self, distracts us and keeps us in the dark for sometimes. Thus, to reach to highest level of enlightenment and tranquility, we should try to rejoin our origin or source of existence by surrendering ourselves to the universal consciousness or internal treasure of presence.

Main negative function of mental self is to create continuous and intense physical, emotional, mental and psychological pains so that we become tired of all these pains and become prepared for a rebirth by jumping and freeing ourselves out of the womb of mental system which causes different types of abnormalities. All these pains are poisons we create within our physical mental, psychological system. However, it is the universal consciousness which pulls the physical and mental consciousness out of the dark prison of our mental system and rejoining it to itself. Although this may look a negative function, but in the long run and after two types of consciousness becomes one with each other, we are free from bondage of our mental system and trouble producing mental self. We are always and simultaneously in a state of happening and becoming within our multi-dimensional existence including our physical, mental, emotional and spiritual dimensions and are also the space that covers all the events or incidents. The same way that the sky with an unlimited space that contains milky way and all the planets, stars, suns, solar systems and heavenly bodies, we have an unlimited space within our internal physical, mental and spiritual system. However, our mental self is very limited and is not able to comprehend the unity and unlimited consciousness.

Mental self or ego always seeks excitement. Mental self has to have excitement to survive. However, it does not matter if excitements are positive or negative. Sometimes mental self tries to engage in dangerous sports such as rock climbing, mountain climbing, bungee jumping, para-shooting, jumping off the cliffs, car racing, boxing, kick boxing, and other forms of fighting or even blood sports to satisfy the thirst for violence and getting excited. These dangerous sports, does not provide people with any real sense of joy but probably releases their rage and stuffed anger. However, people do not obtain any real sense of relaxation or relief. If there is a terrible accident or a horrible situation, people with strong mental self becomes curious and want to know what is happening and like to inform others of these negative event. A good example of paying attention to negative news is different types of media in which people or journalist trying to announce and report a variety of nasty events and even try to exaggerate on it to make it bigger than what really happened. Mental self is addicted to receive bad news. Today with all the available media system this part of mental self's activity becomes even more intense. People, listening or watching the news on TV which only emphasizes on painful events and causes sadness and anger which then, becomes internalized by mental selves. Sadness or happiness in our mental system are only thought processes and are mental concepts. Since both sadness and happiness are contagious, it is better to be happy and influence other people positively by making them happy.

Mental self has a tendency to get angry and store anger, holding grudges and gradually after hoarding all the angers within the mental system it would have a huge amount of stuffed anger that can turn into explosive outburst at any moment. A person with anger creates pain for self and others and as a mental self always search for someone to fight with. It does not matter to whom mental self is fighting, it can be spouse, friend and coworker, whoever who is available at the moment. When we become angry our universal consciousness decreases significantly and our physical mental consciousness of our mental self takes over. Many times over and over the mental self, engages in conflict and fights trying to hurt other people and getting hurt self. Mental self being vengeful and holding grudges, does not let go off the rage and anger and has to get revenge and many times in the process of getting revenge hurt itself and may even destroy self. When snake bit humans, some people instead of getting a fast treatment and neutralize the poison in their body, they go after the snake to get revenge and to kill the snake and waste enough time that poison becomes effective and kill them. Mental self, enjoys to create conflict, quarrel and fight with others either as an individual against another individual or as a member of a group against another group. In order to justify its war mongering affairs, mental self, first try to dehumanize and demonize the other person or group and then it make it easier to justify violence against them and destroy them.

One major characteristic of mental self is fear. Fear is a form of excitement that is caused by our thought influencing our emotional and physical dimension, thus, it is being produced by our fearful mental self. Fear is always attached like a cluster to other forms of fear. The main forms of fear is fear of loss of life, loss of material things and non-material belongings such as our job, role, status, position, power and privilege. The reason behind this type of fear is to consider ourselves as a physical and mental body which will be dying and perishing with anything that we have been co-identified and attached with, some-time in the future. Another reason for having this type of fear is the main characteristics of the mental self which is escaping from the life of this moment and living in the future. Off course the mental self with his/her tendency to escape from the life of this moment and being in a hurry to get to the future, gets conceptually closer to death at any moment. However, if we become aware of our real self as consciousness which is eternal, then, there would not be any reason to be afraid of death or loss of life, or being worried about material belongings or any other worldly thing.

Mental self has an intense degree of jealousy toward other people. A jealous mental self can't see other people to have more than him/her. Concentrating on the idea of the more the better, a person who is jealous also becomes greedy, tries to hoard and add material and non-material belongings to self. The jealous person may be able to get along with people only if he/she has more wealth, money, luxury, house, car or more education, position or status than other people. But if his/her material or non-material belongings become less than others, he/she can't tolerate it and become depressed or angry and try to cause conflict and problem for other people. When a sense of jealousy intensifies in a person because they have something more or better, this person tries to use teasing and trying to bring down the value of what other people have, by making negative remarks about what other people have. We should not react to other people teasing due to their jealousy.

Rumi compares our mental self with a scarecrow or head of a dead animal that farmers used to put in the farm to stop the birds or animals from destroying the crops or the fruits. The scarecrow or the head of a dead animal are just a non-living substance and there is no reason for birds or animal to be afraid of them. However, since the consciousness is still in sleep within the animals, they don't know better. This fear is from unknown items and all the fears that we experience through our mental self are from the unknown. For example, our mental self, which, lives in the future is always afraid that we lose something in the future. The problem arises from the point that the mental self itself is an artificial existence and is afraid of something else that is not based on reality, because future does not exist and always we are the life of this moment. We pick only a few clusters of grapes from the whole harvest of the vineyard or a little seeds from the stack of wheat. By using only a small part of life we can't enjoy the life in its fullness.

Mental self loves misery and always is full of negative emotions such as sadness, depression or anxiety. Mental self always feel sorry for his/her and other people actions. Even when mental self tries to be happy, it is artificial and temporary state and soon goes back to his/her pain addicting self. Part of pain addicting tendency of the mental self relates to attention seeking function of his/her behavior. Our excitement comes out of our emotions. Mental self is full of guilty feelings and self-blames. An anxious person lives in the future and an individual, who is sorry, depressed and feels guilty lives in the past. An individual who always expect others to do things for him/her, becomes codependent with them and loose his/her freedom and independence. Mental self always engages in whining and complaining about life and different issues to let others know he/she is not satisfied and this dissatisfaction in all aspect of life is a major characteristic of mental self. Mental self, concentrating on the future and thinking that future will give him/her a better life is always anxious and worry about the future. When we are sad, depressed with a lot of intense emotional pain we can't be happy and positively influence other people, our work would not be creative or productive. "Once depressed, a set of cognitive distortions exert a general influence over the person's day-to-day functioning. These are manifest as the cognitive triad: negative view of self, current experience, and future" (Hawton, et, al., 1989, P. 11). What we need is the real self with the joy and creativity of the universal consciousness to radiate love, joy and happiness to all directions.

All human miseries, pains and difficulties originates from our mental self that is addicted to pain and suffering. Mental system creates pain through negative thought processes, cognitive distortion, thinking errors and negative excitements including our emotional pains that cover a vast variety of pains. Fear is one of the main negative emotion or excitement in human life, particularly, the fear of loss of one's own life or a loved one, and material belongings, fear of losing a job, position or social status. Chronic sense of fear losing something, keeps the mental self in a constant state of worry and anxiety which comes out of the mental self, trying to live in the future. To have some pain helps us to become mature and experienced and tired of our pain producing mental self, but we should not become addicted to pain. To eliminate the chronic pain of sadness and depression, we should try to understand the nature of depression which is being caused by our mental self, engaging in different types of negative excitements such as internalizing the past pains of hate, revenge, jealousy, high level of expectation, and mistakes. Instead to concentrate on present moment, accept any situation as it is, accept our limitations and forget about the negative events.

Another characteristic of mental self is excessive passion that makes mental self, a slave of un-satiated desires and pulls him/her toward a variety of worldly attractions. Passion is a state that we choose something in the external world, search for life through that thing and become attached to it sometimes to the point of becoming obsessed with it. The excessive passion is the most important negative and destructive characteristic of mental self or ego which does not let mental self to relax and keep it in a constant state of restlessness. The opposite of passion is moral richness, generosity and being free from excessive wants or desires. Excessive passion, distract us from our main goals in life and decreases our concentration and attention for creative work in our daily life. Our mental self is constantly trying to satisfy our passion, while our heart is after love, joy and happiness and rejoining to our lost source. All the movements, activities of all parts of the universe are planned in a way that, lead us to our origin.

Rumi mentions about two types of dreams that mental self, experiences. One is dreaming during our sleep time during the night when our consciousness of presence is active because our mental system and mental self is quiet and inactive. But when morning arrives, we notice what we saw in our dreams during the sleep was not based on reality. Sleep is the time of relaxation and escaping from the bitter reality and the pains and struggles of the external world. When mental self is dreaming we experience nightmare, but when our consciousness is dreaming, it is a pleasant dream. The other form of dreaming occurs during our awake-time which is dreaming within our mental system and the dreamer is mental self, but the content of our dream in this case is negative thought, beliefs, excitements that are being experienced like a chain of disturbing thoughts. The dreamer in both situations during our sleep time and awakes time is the same consciousness and the same observer. But the pleasant dream of sleep time and awake-time comes from the same consciousness, while the nightmare during the night and negative disturbing sleep-like thoughts is experienced by our mental self.

The reason for the day dreaming during our awake-time is that our mental self becomes highly active and engages in perseverative and racing thought processes. Whenever our consciousness is dreaming whether it is during the night or during our awaken time, we experience pleasant dreams, tranquility and creative thought. But whenever, our mental self is dreaming, we experience nightmares during our sleep and we experience negative and disturbing thought during our awaken time. Our mental system is constantly dreams in a sleep-like state and is distracted from the real essence and purpose of our living life. What is important to us and is a major responsibility for us is to be awakened from the sleep of our mental system. If we are awaken from the sleep of our mental system, then, we become really awaken and can experience universal consciousness and enlightenment. We as human mental selves create our own thoughts and beliefs then we give it life and then we become co-identified and attached to them. Gradually the mental construct of our mental system becomes a demon or evil which in turn control us.

Mental self has a tendency to control other people. For example parents as mental selves try to control their children thinking that they know everything and their children should follow exactly what they dictate. The danger of this type of control is that children become too dependent on parents and lose their freedom and independence. The result is co-dependency which is a sick type of social relationship. Any time a person with strong mental self tries to control other people, it causes real problem for them. Controlling a group, society or nation will turn into dictatorship and an oppressive type of relationship. We should understand that all people like to be free and independent including members of our family. Thus, it is better to provide everyone around us with their freedom and independence. All humans feel free and self-confident when they are being treated with dignity and respect without someone else trying to control them.

Mental self has a pattern of criticizing and fault finding that is conducive to creating conflict with others. By criticizing others, mental self tries to make self, flawless and more important. The first people who tried to use their mental self were Adam and Eve. By using mental system they became attached and co-identified by their thought and belief and worldly things. Adam used the first thinking error of finding fault in Eve and accused her of misleading him to eat the forbidden fruit. Mental self does not accept the responsibility of his/her action and blame others for any type of wrong doing, but hides his/her own mistakes. Mental self is always suspicious of other people and does not trust others. Mental self, working within the limited mental system, can't comprehend why things happens and always looks for a reason for events or incidents and try to find a cause for any event that occurs. In fact nothing is directly the cause of something else. Finding a cause is a mental work trying to make sense of external reality. Many events that happens in the external environment, does not have external cause. Similar events may happen simultaneously in two different places or at two different points in time. Mental self being made of artificial and distorted cloud of darkness itself, is suspicious of all other people and does not have any real basis for existence. Consciousness that resides within everything and every human being can make it possible for two people to create the same or similar idea or invention simultaneously or at two different points in time.

This suspiciousness will continue as long as mental self is active and in operation. The suspiciousness will end when the mental self becomes weak, inactive and dissolved. Then, the real self takes over. Mental self tries to become friend with another mental self who he/she perceives as an important person only to make self, important and then tries to destroy that person to become even more important. Mental self gets its fuel from causing conflict and fighting with other people. Being an artificial and temporary self, a mental self, creates a fight to establish self and become more aware of his/her existence. When someone says something no matter what the content of his/her speech is, the mental self takes a defensive approach and react impulsively by attacking the other person. The wrong assumption of mental self is that other people are causing problem for the mental self, but it is the mental self itself that is causing problems for self and others and creates conflict. The suspiciousness, paranoia, delusions and confusion of mental self intensifies when the deficient reason and logic of mental self is not to comprehend the external reality as it is. This happens when mental self's picture or perception of external reality does not match with the external reality itself.

Mental self has a tendency to work without pay meaning that mental self, engages in affairs which wastes time with no benefit. Examples of work without pay are using anger, bad temper, threat as well as put down and blaming the children while trying to teach them. Group also can engage in work without pay. Examples are group fighting, wars, revolution, destruction and causing pain for another group. Nation, society, and country which goes to war with another nation, country or society, their mental selves are at work trying to create more pains for other mental selves. No one is real winner in the wars. Both sides are losers. Conflict and wars are the failure of human groupings to use their real selves and instead, they let their internal evil or mental selves to take over and cause pain for everyone.

Rumi, in his poems identifies four birds that he considers as symbols of our negative excitements, emotions, and attachment or co-identification with worldly attractions. These birds are: 1. Duck, is considered as a symbol of an un-satiated greed and intense wants of material wealth, 2. Peacock, is considered as a symbol of grandiosity and peacock's feathers are a means of pride, bragging, seeking attention and showing off, 3. Rooster, is considered as a symbol of intense sexual desires, and 4. Robin, is considered as a symbol of desiring a long life which can be miserable and painful. Rumi believes that unless we destroy these nasty internal birds which are symbols of four main types of greed, we will not be free from the negative excitements and misery of these types of attachments. To live a short joyful, relaxed and rich life is better than having a miserable long life in an uncertain future. Grandiosity and pride as feelings makes mental self to see self, better and more important than others and do not respect others. Revenge is considered a vicious wolf or dog that create an internal fire that destroy and tear apart the human from within and when it becomes old, it turns into a major vengefulness that like fires burns human internally. We should differentiate between desires of our mental system and the desires of our real self: 1. Desires of mental self which is psychological and artificial needs such as being accepted, approved, respected etc. and 2.Desires of our real self or consciousness which are creativity, abundance, beauty and tranquility.

Mental self, trying to escape from life of this moment is always impatient, restless, and in a hurry to go to the future, thinking that future will bring success and happiness. Constant hurrying is one of the characteristics of mental self. "Impatience and constant hurrying are both aspects of a general attitude that is called time urgency. It is if the chronically angry person is in a time pressure cooker." (Bruno,1993, p. 23). Mental self is bored most of the times and nothing make it happy and amused, thus, trying to go to the future with the hope of a better situation or condition. This is because mental self is never satisfied with life of this moment and nothing is enough because, mental self likes to hoard material things and luxuries that he/she may not have at present time, thus, try to hoard and add something more to self. Bruno distinguished between two forms of boredom. "Situational boredom is specific, and everyone has experienced it… Chronic boredom is general and pervasive…" (Bruno, P. 37) Mental self, experiences both forms of boredom.

V

Negative Functions of Mental System and Mental Self: A Source of Cognitive Distortion and Suffering

"The Devil is hidden beneath outward form. When he finds no form at hand, he enters your thoughts, to cause them to draw you into sin. From your thoughts proceeds destructions, when from time to time evil thoughts occur to you... Ah! Cast out oOf your head these evil suggestions. Ah! Sweep out of your heart these evil suggestions. Cry, "There is no power, nor strength but in God! To avert the Evil one from the world and your soul (Rumi, 13th Century) (Translated from Persian into English by: Whinfield, 1898, P. 49, 50)

Rumi believes that human mental self, possesses a pattern of resistance, combativeness and negative clusters of thought and beliefs and opinions. Our mental self is full of cognitive distortion, negative excitements, erroneous beliefs, thinking errors, and old and biased ideas we inherited from our parents and predecessors. This condition create limitation in our free thinking, then, we have a choice of staying in the prison of our mental system or jumping out of it and achieving the second birth. Mental self keeps us depressed, fearful, angry, guilty and aggressive, and paralyzes our brain and related thinking patterns. Then, it is necessary to reduce, weaken and even destroy our biased mental self or ego. Instead we should develop our real and objective self which is in line and parallel to real life processes and events. Cognitive distortion and thinking errors are characteristics of mental self. However, the right comprehension, thinking, and right deeds, as well as right decision making and the right action are major characteristics of universal consciousness which thinks, and works through us to achieve, joy, happiness, relaxation and creativity. Thought is one form of mental disease. Co-identification with thought, belief, opinion and excitement creates different kinds of disorders in all our dimensions including physical, mental, psychological, emotional and spiritual dimensions. The disease of spiritual dimension is when we produce a mental god, life and consciousness which is only a concept and not based on any reality.

Mental system only works with duality. Thus, the mental self is based on duality of life and has to have two opposites or complementary phenomena or things to compare and something to fight with. Again according to our historical and religious information we received from our ancestors, Adam and Eve were the first people to engage in duality of life and began using their mental system and see each other as opposite sex, being ashamed of the differences of their genitals, they covered their genital area with the fig leaves. Mental self makes sense of external reality through contrasts and everything has two sides to it. For example concentrating about past and future, mental self is not able to take advantage of the present. Duality comes from deficient eyesight of mental self that is working through mental system and sees everything with the dark glasses and only becomes aware of things as opposites not as complementary or as one unit.

Mental self is made of thought, beliefs and excitements. The distance between two thoughts or beliefs or excitements is life itself. Thus thoughts and beliefs are distractions and diversion from living life. Within each frame of thought, belief or excitement a different self, emerges. Thoughts, beliefs and excitements are not dangerous by themselves, but to become attached and show impulsive reaction to those thoughts, beliefs and excitement are troublesome and dangerous. Mental self always lives in psychological times of the past and the future. At any moment we may escape from the life of this moment and fall into the trap of mental system and renew our mental self. Mental self is not able to comprehend unity, because mental system works through duality and comparing opposites such as white and black; day and night; past and present; up and down; right and left; rich and poor; I and you; we and them; hot and cold, etc. Since real, objective, original self is based on unity, then, metal self is not aware of this type of unity and can't comprehend the eternal, unlimited, formless existence of total consciousness.

Mental self, acts based on old beliefs, thoughts, opinions and ideas internal-ized and transferred to us by our parents and predecessors which are mostly incompatible with contemporary ideas and life style. Thoughts and ideas can serve positive functions but, we should not be addicted to them or to become co-identified with them. Rumi says that consciousness has become separated from matter in human, thus we should not let it to stay in our mental system for a long time. As human beings, to live normally and be happy, we should let our total consciousness to be our leads, not the deficient reason and logic of our mental self. Based on our past experiences with negative events we may react negatively to any current event or incident. However, we should be aware that any time we show impulsive reaction based on our old habits to an event or incident, we experience intense excitement and emotional, psychological pain. If we are able not to show any reaction to the events and not to resist and fight with it, we will stand above it and we will not suffer because of those incidents.

According to Rumi, when a thought comes to our mind and mental self, it stays in our brain for a long time and can cause other disturbing thoughts. It does not matter if we try to escape that thought by trying to change our location and travel to a different place. The thought particularly negative and disturbing thought will follow us no matter where we go. Since our mental self is the agent of mental system, the best way to stop the negative thought process is to deactivate and make our mental system and mental self, quiet by concentrating on our real self or consciousness that is full of love and joy. Because any form of pain is occurring in our mental system, thus, instead of physically moving from one place to another, we should get out of our mental system and jump into our realm of consciousness and unity deep within ourselves. The more deep we go within the time of this moment, the more we become of the same quality of our origin or universal consciousness. Our universal consciousness is also the universal intelligence which extends into our body and mind and becomes a physical mental system and creates the mental self only to be able to experience the external world. We should not resist and let the universal consciousness and intelligence to work through us and makes us creative and joyfull.

Mental self, possesses a cluster of negative and disturbing thought process. One of the elements of the cluster is a wrong conception of time. Mental self always lives either in the past, or in the future not paying attention to the present time at this moment. Past and present are only thought, mental construct and concepts made by our mental self and are not based on reality. Thus yesterday and tomorrow do not exist at this moment. It is always this moment that is real. By concentrating on the future events, and thinking that future will bring happiness and joy of life, the mental self is always in a hurry to reach to the future, thus, does not enjoy the present life situations. By escaping from the life of this moment which is the main real aspects of our life, mental self always escape from the life of this moment into the past and present which are mental concepts without any tangible reality. Our life is occurring at this moment and always it is this moment when we can enjoy life and be relaxed. The life in the past occurred at this moment and the life of the future when arrives will occur at this moment.

The psychological time of the future is associated with pain because mental self sees the life in the future and that is impossible. All the people who tried to talk about a utopia they made it in their mental system and talked about a society in the future that could be ideal and perfect including the paradise. Thomas Moore and Karl Marx and Plato all talked about utopia or ideal society of the future in their mental system. They were living in the future and they did not like their societies of their time but none of those societies became possible. Life exists only at this moment but not in the future. The only thing about the future, that exist for mental self is the concept of anxiety which is an emotion caused by mental construct of the unknown future. Even a curse or talisman is supposed to do something bad to someone in the future. Many people do not enjoy their life of this moment with the hope of experiencing a better life in the future or in a different place. As long as we are alive and have our pain producing mental self with us, it does not matter where we are and what psychological time it is. We continue to experience pain and suffering produced by our mental self.

To think about the future does not mean that we have to forget the present time. We should not live in the future or rely on the unknown future at present time, because it only causes anxiety and worries. In order to live at this moment, we should cut the chain of thoughts that does not let us concentrate at the life of this moment and thus, we lose our present moment. The life of this moment which is "to be" should be connected and converted to the life of the future which will be "to become." However even to become can occur at this moment because we can only experience the future at this moment. Life always is at this moment. When our mental system becomes simple and empty, the psychological time disappears, and the negation of time occurs. The negation of time occurs simultaneously with the negation of our mental self and brings us to the life of this moment. Then, we see ourselves as life of this moment and experience a sense of unity with consciousness.

According to Rumi, a person who is trapped within the concept of psychological time and only think about the past and the future has a dead heart and is a being, that lives in the past and suffer because of the old negative events but his/her eyes are concentrated toward the future where he/she expects to gain something. There is no real past or future at any moment. There is only one unit of time which is this moment and it is constant. The past, future and this moment are all the same. It is only the events, incidents, situations and conditions that are happening at this moment that we experience. However, we should not identify ourselves with those events or situations. It is our mental self that is limited to understand everything based on the past, present and the future. A person who lives in the past and all his hopes are in the future, is positioned him/herself in between the real objective self or real life of presence and the external world and by using the deficient reason of his/her mental self is far from the presence and with no fire of love and joy of life. Any mental self who tries to go against the flow of the evolution of consciousness, will reach to a dead end and destruction which actually facilitate the process of physical and mental consciousness to jump out of the bondage of our mental system and its agent mental self.

The only reason we always think about the past and the present is because our mental system is limited and only works through duality and has to compare everything. Even our language is based on the duality of the past, and future which we add to our present. Linear time with all the corresponding incidents and events is confusing and entrap the human beings within the events of the past or make them anxious about the unknown events of the future. Time has been internalized within our mental system as a relative phenomenon because living in our planet and experiencing the day and night due to the earth revolving around itself and around the sun. Thus, causing the day and night as two parts of the time. If we travel outside of the atmosphere of this planet there would be only day all the time and it makes it easier to understand the present time and this moment, instead of seeing time as the past or the future which is caused by the movement of earth and the psychological time within our mental system.

To Rumi, three demons that constantly steal our attention and get us to cause problem for self and others are: 1. Resisting consciousness, 2. Wrong judgement, and 3. Attachment or co-identification and co-dependency with our thoughts, beliefs, opinions, excitements and material world. Mental self always over-estimates his/her skills, knowledge and power and thinks he/she knows everything and has an opinion about every aspect of life, even-though it does not have enough knowledge about anything. Thinking that his/her knowledge is more than others, mental self, under-estimate others and is eager to change others and concentrate on other peoples' short coming and is blind to her/his deficiencies and incompleteness. By over-estimating self and under-estimating others, the mental self thinks he/she is always right and others are always wrong. Thus, closes the window of learning new knowledge and information.

Mental self does not follow the code of appropriate communication and politeness. His/her speech is full of negative, critical and disrespectful remarks toward others. Disrespecting others can happen both, in front of other people or behind their back. Mental self likes to talk about people behind their back. By putting other people down and making them smaller and bad, mental self tries to make self, more important and better than others. Talking about other people also serves the function of showing self as someone who knows more than others. The mental self, thinking that everybody else is wrong and he/she is right, never listens to other people and never learn as long as continues to talk non-stop and not to listen to what they may have to offer. When we are in a gathering and people are talking about a subject, a person with a strong mental self can't stay quiet and has to say something to prove it to other people that he/she knows more than them. What happens is that our mental self, become unleashed and out of our control and try to impress others and intensify his/her wrong pride, grandiosity and narcissism. Mental self, puffs up like a cat to show that we are bigger than what we really are.

Mental self has a pattern of illogical expectation, approval and respect which if it is not unmet, can turn into feeling rejected, sad and unhappy. Mental self makes self, recognized and important through creating conflict and quarrel with others. Mental self makes self, puffed up and maintain him/herself through conflict, argument, and fighting with others. Thus, conflict, contrast and control is the main motivation in dealing with others. Mental self likes to control everybody and expect them to do whatever, he/she wishes. Skinner (1971, 1972) believed that" the controlling self generally represents the interest of others, the controlled self the interest of the individual". (Skinner, P.190).

Mental self, likes to be respected and approved by others and does not tolerate any disapproval, disrespect or rejection by others.

Rumi believes that trying to be approved by others is like hunting flies. It is a waste of time and a work without pay. Evaluating ourselves with our mental self we consider ourselves as mentally and physically sick, but when we evaluate ourselves by the knowledge of our consciousness, we really experience a joyful and healthy life. Mental system is a passage of stormy wind which mental self is creating and destroying us. To be safe from this storm, we should be in the presence of our universal consciousness and out of our mental system. Mental self has to have approval of other people to be certain that it has an existence. Mental self loves to hear good things about self. The more good things people say about mental self, the more important he/she feels and the more grandiose he/she becomes.

Rumi believes that resistance is one of the major characteristic of mental self. Mental self has a rigid frame of mind and is resistant to anything that he/she does not approve. Mental self through obsessive-compulsive thought process and rigidity of his/her belief system develops a frame of mind that is very rigid and evaluate everything within that framework. Thus, anything that is not in line with his/her framework is not acceptable to the metal self. No matter how much resistance mental self uses to maintain its infrastructure, the process of the evolution of consciousness after maturity of the consciousness within the mental system will diminish and weakens the mental self and help releasing the trapped consciousness from the mental system which becomes one with the universal consciousness.

Rumi Referring to pharaoh and Moses story, explains that when Pharaoh tried to resist and not to follow Moses recommendation of believing to the God or consciousness, Moses through his stick on the floor which turned into a dragon or huge snake eating snakes of the Pharaoh's magicians. Rumi considers Moses stick a symbol of consciousness that swallowed the mental self of Pharaoh and his followers. Moses tells Pharaoh, you have mountain snake, but the snake of the sky and the realm of unity or consciousness eats you and your followers. In addition to the snake as consciousness, Moses turned the water in the river Nile into blood for Pharaoh and his followers, but for followers of Moses water was clean and clear. Again water is considered as symbol of consciousness.

Mental self has a pattern of comparing self with others which creates many problems such as a sense of jealousy, a sense of grandiosity or a sense of inferiority. This pain producing activity of mental self which is comparing self to others, usually produce two types of problems. One is finding out that the mental self does not have the same things that others have which causes jealousy and a sense of being lower than others, thus, developing a sense of inferiority and losing self confidence and self-esteem, and the other is when mental self thinks he/she has more money, wealth, education, prestige, status, position than others, therefore, developing a sense of grandiosity and superiority over others. By comparing self to others and the philosophy of obtaining as much as possible, or the more the better, a person becomes greedy and can never be satisfied in life. Greed or an un-satiated wants is a major pain producing trait of the mental self, which gives the mental self an entitlement to take money, land, and other properties of others without any feeling of remorse. The problem with the un-satiated wants or greed of the mental self is that the more things a greedy person takes from others, the more thirsty, he/she becomes for more things. And then, works even harder to add to what he/she already has but not through the right means, but through fraudulent activities. The main philosophy of the mental self is the more the better.

Mental self also has a pattern of searching for a sense of security and maintenance. For mental self to maintain its artificial and transitory existence, it is necessary to have another mental self to compare, to have conflict with, to criticize, to put down, to blame and to control. It is through impulsive reaction and interaction with another mental self, a mental self tries to maintain self. A mental self always is worry because of concentrating on the unknown future and what future may bring him/her. Thus, worries about loss of life, loss of jobs, loss of personal material and non-material belongingness such as power, privilege, role, status, and artificial reputation. In reality all of these material and non-material things are temporary and perishable and we can't be really sure to have a real sense of security, if it is our mental self who is searching for it. Our real sense of security comes from our consciousness that is permanent, eternal, unlimited, timeless and formless. As consciousness we always live at present not the future or the past, thus we will never lose anything because of our formlessness, timelessness, and being eternal, permanent and unlimited.

Mental self wants to obtain everything easy and does not believe that we have to work right and hard to gain something. The engine of wants in mental self never stops and there is no satiation point to be satisfied. Thus, the mental self is always dissatisfied no matter how much money, wealth or other belongings he/she possesses. In order to reach to a treasure of any kind, we have to work hard and be persistent to obtain it. In order to reach to the right end, mental self, uses wrong means and whatever activity necessary to reach to that end. This evil tendency of mental self, empowers a person to take the money, property or land and other belongings of other people and entitle self to possess things that belongs to others. This orientation also is a major cause of jealousy. It is the materialism and tendency toward luxury and material belongings under the influence of advertising that brings us under the bondage of materialism. Similar to Rumi, Buddha asks that "Where is, lamentation, pain and agony? It is not to be found in the fact that people are generally desirous. They cling obstinately to lives of wealth and honor, comfort and pleasure, excitement and self-indulgence, ignorant of the fact that the desire for these very things is the source of human suffering." (Kyokai, 1966, P.42,43).

Mental self, acting within mental system, has to become co-identified and co-dependent with his/her belongings such as material things, money, luxury, house, car, position, thought, beliefs, opinions, excitements, mental, psychological and physical pains and thus develops a strong sense of ownership. Mental self always thinks he/she is incomplete and wants to add something to self, whether it is material items or status, privilege and power. Mental self which feels to be deficient tries to show that he/she is more important, better and higher than anybody else. This sense of grandiosity causes a social relationship based on an unequal status in which the mental self, expect others to respect him/her. Mental self expects everybody to appreciate him/her for anything he/she does. This tendency will create a high level of expectation from others and thus, will stay dissatisfied in his/her life for the rest of his/her life.

When we intensely attach ourselves to material or non-material things, we develop a sense of ownership. Thinking that getting attached to other people or belongings makes us more complete, our mental self, search for other people and material things to add something to self and look more complete and important. Recognizing our attachment and co-identification with material life helps us to become detached and free ourselves from the bondage of co-identification. If we have a strong sense of ownership on any material object or person or a role, position, status, power and privilege, we become very angry and disappointed when we lose those belongings. Experiencing a strong sense of ownership and entitlement also leads to greed and excessive wants and desires that becomes un-satiated and problematic for a person.

The more we expand and glorify our mental self, the less our real, objective, original self becomes clear to us. We create a cloud of darkness and hide our spiritual and real self. When this situation arises, the real self does not work to provide us with tranquility, joy and happiness, creativity and productivity, instead our mental self, acts up by creating all kinds of negative excitements and physical, mental and emotional pain. The main reason our mental self makes many mistakes is because mental self sees the world through the dark glasses and see everything distorted. We should be a bright and clear mirror of total consciousness so that the ray of knowledge, tranquility, and joy of life to be radiated by us and through us to the external world. Using our mental self we only radiate excitements, negative emotions, negative thinking and old beliefs and pains to the external world. Radiating the negative excitement of rage, anger, revengefulness, fear, pain and suffering negatively affect all other mental selves and we will have a society of people who are unhealthy, unhappy and depressed.

Not being able to experience the joy and happiness of our universal consciousness, the mental self always follow a pattern of anger, rage, fury and violence. Mental self gets its identification and make self, important through conflict and combativeness. This is based on what mental self considers self and what he/she considers others. Since the major identification of mental self can be achieved through conflict, then, mental self needs others to quarrel with. But sometimes, a mental self, joins other mental selves to create an in-group so that they can identify an out-group to fight with. The thinking error that mental self, possesses is based on the assumption that anything inside the group is positive and acceptable, and anything related to the out-group is bad and unacceptable. Sometimes mental selves exaggerate to the point that they demonize the member of the out group to facilitate and make their violence against them justified. Even animals do not have the rage, violence, and vengefulness that human have. Animal kills to eat food that is necessary for their survival, but human kills each other because of their paranoia, fear, wrong judgement, and many other cognitive distortions. People hold grudges and try to hurt other people sometimes individually and sometimes as a group.

One major characteristic of mental self that create separation and social distance between two people is artificial pride which is based on a person's wrong perception, thinking or belief. A person who have artificial pride, think of him/herself superior, better, richer, prettier, more powerful or stronger or more important than others. Thus, this person relate to others based on unequal social relationship and exchange. Artificial pride is a disease of the mind and a conflict producing factor among people. This cognitive distortion leads to an artificial sense of grandiosity, showing off and bragging which produces social distance between the person and others around him/her. Rumi believes that we should accept our responsibility if we do anything wrong and to be aware that all our miseries are related to our own action and not actions of other people.

Rumi asks himself "who am I that I don't have any obsession or compulsion or the arousal of disturbing thoughts in my mind and I am being pulled to this way and that way." Then, he answers himself and says "It is because I am made of consciousness not the racing thought of my mind and mental system." Obsessions comes from the nature of our mental self that evaluates itself based on external phenomena and creates a sense of fear, greed and insecurity of life and constantly is in fear of losing his/her temporary transitory material belongings. Obsession is a state of being constantly pulled to different directions by our racing thought processes. The solution to our obsessions is to follow our consciousness not our disturbing thoughts. Consciousness is in sleep in solids, plants and animals. However, consciousness in human beings is awake and aware. Rumi says I am not selling myself in the market of selling self but the market of selling love. Matter is not my origin, my real origin and essence is consciousness which can't be sold. Some people sell themselves in the market of materialism. We can dissolve all of our negative thoughts, beliefs, opinions, and excitements only through our love and consciousness.

Mental self is always dissatisfied with life and complains, cries, and criticizes everybody and everything at any moment. Mental self finds any excuses to show that life is not worth living. When, the weather is warm mental self, complaints about heat, if the weather is too cold, mental self, complaints about cold. No matter which season it is mental self is not happy and complaints about any natural phenomena such as spring, fall, winter, and summer. One of the major complains of mental self is to grow old and lose beauty, youth and most of his/her abilities and skills. With this wrong expectation, mental self always takes a victim stance and complains not knowing that aging is a natural process of dissolving our body and deactivating mental self and getting prepared for the freedom of our consciousness from the prison of our body and mental system. Thus, human is going toward silence and being freed from excessive thinking and talking of mental self.

Many psychologists discussed about cognitive distortion and thinking errors that affects our emotions and behaviors. Ellis (1977); Beck (1976); Horney,

(1950); Fromm (1966, 1983); Thomas (1923); Tussing (1959); Goode (1984); Dollard and Miller (1950); Rotter (1954, 1981, 1982); Beck (1976, 1999) and many more. McKay and McKay (1989) in their book "When anger hurts," described several thinking errors which they considered as "Trigger thoughts". According to Thomas (1923) developed the concept of "the definition of situation," According to him "a person's cognitive view of himself, other people and the world influences his/her behavior." Fromm's concept of "Transference is very similar to Thomas's "the definition of the situation." "Transference," is probably one of the most common reasons for human error and conflict in seizing up reality. It makes us see the world through the glasses of our own wishes and fears and consequently makes us confuse illusion with reality" (1983, PP. 78, 79). Beck (1976) provided a list of six major erroneous thinking patterns. Freeman & Dewolf, in their book entitled "woulda, coulda, shoulda," listed fifteen thinking errors (1990, P. 59).

The mental self is being established through thinking and talking and will be dissolved through silence and concentration and meditation. Anything in this world that we consider important will become unimportant and nondesirable very fast, because our mental self is always dissatisfied no matter what, he/she adds or hoards. Thought process within our mental system can be so rapid and can go round and round twirling in our mind that can cause confusion and dizziness when we try to stop our active mental self. Our racing thought in the mental system causes the same effect as twirling around ourselves for a while and then, suddenly stop can cause the state that we experience the whole environment moving around us. But this is just a delusion not based on reality.

According to Rumi it is our thoughts, beliefs and excitements or emotions that are created within our mental system by our mental selves that is cause of our wrong doings, pain and suffering that we create for ourselves and others and that no one else is responsible for our actions but ourselves. In line with Rumi's idea about the negative thinking patterns of mental self, Yokelson & Samenow, introduced the concept of "Errors in thinking" and listed many thinking errors. They took a revolutionary approach and declared that individuals are responsible for their misbehavior. As Samenow puts it "Criminals cause crime—not bad neighborhood, inadequate parents, television, schools, drugs, or unemployment. Crime resides within the minds of human beings and is not caused by social conditions." (Samenow, 1984, p. 6). Some of the negative thought and beliefs mentioned in the long list of thinking errors explained by Yokelson & Samenow are similar to the evil characteristics of mental self within the mental system explained by Rumi 800 years ago.

An extensive and exhaustive list of thinking errors, were identified by Yokelson & Samenow (1976). They explained many Thinking errors characteristics of the criminal and criminal thinking patterns that leads to criminal and deviant behaviors including: energy; fear; zero state; anger; pride; the power trust; sentimentality; religion; concrete thinking; fragmentation; uniqueness; perfectionism; suggestibility; the loner; sexuality and lying (pp. 251-348). They also identified automatic error of thinking such as: closed channel; "I Can't"; the victim stance; lack of time perspective; failure to put oneself in another's position; failure to consider inquiry to others; failure to assume obligation; failure to assume responsible initiatives; ownership; fear of fear; lack of trust; refusal to be dependent; lack of interest in responsible performance; pretentiousness; failure to make effort or endure adversity; poor decision making for responsible living (pp. 359-401). Yokelson & Samenow identified many other criminal thinking errors regarding extensiveness of criminal thinking such as: Deterrents; corrosion and cut off; build up the opinion of oneself as good; deferment; super-optimism; emergence of nonpsychotic hallucinatory deterrents; reemergence of fear during the execution of the crime; when the criminal remain un-apprehended; celebration after the crime; the criminal apprehended; the psychology of accountability; premeditation vs. impulse-compulsion; the effectiveness of deterrents (pp. 407-453).

VI

Universal Consciousness and Love: A source of Joy and Happiness

"Looking at my life I see that only love has been my soul's companion. From deep inside my soul cries out: Do not wait, surrender for the sake of love." (Rumi, 13ᵗʰ Century), Translated from Persian into English by Mafi & Kolin (1999, p. 7)

According to Rumi, all forms of love and attractions of all forms are extension of love of universal consciousness within the forms. Love of other human beings, love of animals, love of plants and flowers and even all the beautiful mountains, valleys, forests, deserts, rivers, lakes, seas, oceans and the beautiful blue sky with the sun and the moon, and all other plants and stars are attraction of universal consciousness within all these forms. Among people love of the lover, fatherly love, motherly love, brotherly love and sisterly love as well as love of children are different forms of love which again is the love of consciousness from one body to the consciousness in another body or form. When we fall in love with another person it is not the physical appearance or the beauty of another person on the surface but the consciousness within all humans can fall in love and attracted to the same kind of consciousness or itself in another body or form. Thus, when two human beings or couples are making love with each other, the power of consciousness of a man and the power of consciousness of a woman are making love with each other. It is the love of life to another life. But, the love of one mental self to another is only sexual and physical attraction and is based on sexual passion.

When the life force intensifies in us, plays us like a musical instrument. It plays the note of our madness and love. The note of our mental self's reason is the note of our misery, control, slavery and artificial self-importance. We should live with our real life self, the lion but not our mental self, the internal wolf. We sometimes fight with our self and sometimes without self. This means that our mental self is in conflict with our real self. No human being is without mental self. It is impossible not to have a mental self. However, having a mental self, serving a mixed positive and negative function of producing pain and suffering and thus, pushing us out of the hell of mental system, where we can rejoin the universal consciousness. Rumi addressing human as consciousness says that we are the moon that can't be contained in the unlimited sky and moving planets and stars and we are water that can't be contained in the ocean. This is to show that our mental system does not have the capacity to comprehend the unlimited realm of unity and our origin. If we be able to know our real self, then we will know our origin. Rumi addressing human says that you are an angel and a creature which can't be stored or contained within a store of mental system for ever. What can be stored in the mental system are our pains and sufferings.

All our dimensions such as our mental system and thoughts, physical system, spiritual system soul, and consciousness are interconnected and through their interactions we experience different forms of positive or negative excitements and emotional state. Being attached and co-identified and codependent with existence provides us with artificial soul and our psychological, emotional and mental pains converts into physical pains or conversely, our physical pains in turn can make us emotionally disturbed and psychologically and mentally imbalanced. However, our consciousness is a control valve that intervenes and creates a balance when we are experiencing imbalance or disequilibrium in our daily life. Our reason and logic can't help us when we are imbalanced. The only thing that is effective is our consciousness and love. If we become unaware of unity and oneness with our consciousness then we cause pain and sufferings for ourselves and others. But becoming one with consciousness we feel joyful and transfer our joy and tranquility through love to other people.

Rumi addressing the humans and asks their consciousness and says my love how long you have to stay in the strange land of mental system where you only see the reflection of things. Return from this strange land and go to your permanent realm of unity, how long you want to be sad. Rumi believes that the consciousness can't stay in the dark prison of mental system for a long time and has to get out. At each moment we receive a message from the universal consciousness that invite us to join it. We either do not read the message or ignore it because we are busy with collecting and hoarding material objects and luxuries and are amused with different kinds of distractions in life. But nothing of this world can give us happiness and joy for a long time. After a short while, we become bored and tired of material belongings because our joy and happiness does not relate to the things of the external world, but joy and happiness comes from our within or from our consciousness. Consciousness is aware of our situations at all moments and constantly works on us to free us. All creatures in the universe consciously or unconsciously are dancing by the power of love of consciousness but, while plants and animal's consciousness is instinctual, human consciousness is consciousness of presence a pure consciousness. All movement of the particles of the universe is in the process of constant motion and dance.

According to Rumi consciousness becomes separated from the matter in human body but has to stay for a short while in order to experience the world through human. We don't need to obtain life from the external world. We are life ourselves, but should not stay in the trap of physical body, mental system and the external world for an extended time. The material life is the life of our mental self. However, our real life is our consciousness. The real love song we sing is the song of creativity, affection and spreading beauty and the life giving energy to the whole world. Consciousness within human body and mental self is restless and tries to get out of mental system as soon as possible. When human dances and moves, it is the consciousness that moves the body and is trying to fly out of the body. Love is a state that self, separates and free itself from the attachments and co-identification or co-dependency. Love becomes possible within the life of this moment which unifies us with our origin. The real lovers are those people who became consciously awaken from the sleep of their mental system and operate within the realm of unity.

Rumi talks about a lover who was very persistent to meet his beloved. The beloved sends him a message to come and see me in a special time and place. The lover waits but before the beloved come, he goes to sleep. The beloved cuts parts of his sleeve and puts a few walnuts in his pocket meaning that you are not mature and qualified to act like an adult lover, and that you are sleep within your mental system. Thus, you can play with walnuts, the games children used to play in the past. Walnut is considered a symbol of worldly item that people gets attached to. Consciousness within forms including humans, are at different stage of evolutionary process. In some people, consciousness reaches the highest possible level for that person and it is possible that he/she is at the stage of presence and oneness with consciousness and in some people it is at lower stage of evolution. It is only a matter of time that all humans will reach to the stage of presence.

Both Mental self and Consciousness of presence as extension of universal consciousness are residing within us and work through us as human being. But while mental self is a temporary and artificial reflection of consciousness of presence and establishes a temporary physical mental consciousness, the consciousness of presence as an extension of universal consciousness is our origin. Mental self as a conglomeration of thoughts, beliefs, and excitements is supposed to exist temporarily and during a short period of time enough to provide us with our experiences and recognition of our environmental phenomena. This mental self gradually should be dissolved and become smaller and let the trapped consciousness within the mental system to be freed and join the universal consciousness. However, through resistance, suspiciousness and separation, mental self as a physical and mental consciousness leads to a rigid sense of ego with its cluster of thought, belief, opinions and excitements which in turn causes physical emotional and psychological pain. This rigid system of mental self is not really representative of our real self and consciousness.

According to Rumi, at any time in our life, two types of conscious selves are at work. One is the real self and the other one is the mental self. We should observe and be aware of our own behavior to see if it is our mental self which is acting out or it is our real self that is operating through us. Whenever we engage in evil, deviant, abnormal, maladaptive, destructive, harmful, criminal behavior or act based on our thinking errors, cognitive distortion, or excitement of our negative emotions such as fear, anger, rage and combativeness, it is the evil mental self or ego that is operating within us which causes conflict, pain and suffering. But whenever, we engage in positive, constructive, creative, helpful behavior, it is our real self or consciousness, which is operating through us, and thus, creating, joy, happiness, creativity, prosperity, tranquility, for us and everybody around us. Our real self or the consciousness of presence is always observing and is aware of what our deviant and evil mental self is doing. However, all the pain that our mental self or ego is creating for us is helping to speed up the process of the evolution of our consciousness within our mental system and facilitates the freedom of consciousness from the bondage of our mental system.

Zoroaster and Buddha were the first two people who realized that humans are made of consciousness as their main essence. Rumi says that we human as consciousness convert the pains or stings of bees into sweet syrup and honey that comes from the energy of consciousness in the realm of "to be or unity." Within the realm of unity all human beings love each other. To be is the origin and life tries to convert us to "to be." To have is equivalent of adding and hoarding, a characteristic of our mental self, but to be is the reality of our existence. This energy makes us selfless and converts us to pure consciousness. The sting is symbol of pain and the honey is the symbol of consciousness of presence. The same analogy exist between mental self as a deficient, artificial and transitory being which tries to make self, perfect thus, talking about going through a path of perfection and becoming a perfect human being which is nothing but a thought within the mental system.

Rumi believes that all parts of the universe are interrelated and interconnected to each other and consciousness within all parts of the universe connects all the creatures and forms with each other and unites everything like cement. Thus Consciousness or God is perfect essence within everything. The only perfect being within us is the eternal, formless, timeless and unlimited consciousness and is not really completely separate from us at any moment. Thus, our obligation is to recognize our origin and become aware of our real essence. We don't need to go through any path to reach God or consciousness. We are the perfect being as consciousness. Descartes also stated that "It also occurs to me that whenever we ask whether the works of God are perfect, we should examine the whole universe together and not just one creature in isolation from the rest. Something, if all by itself, may rightfully appear very imperfect; but if it is seen in its role as a part in the universe, it is most perfect." (Descartes,1979, P. 36).

Rumi considers the mental self as a physical mental consciousness, a form of consciousness that is trapped within our mental system. He compares this with water and dirt which creates mod. Water represents the consciousness trapped in the mod which represents our mental system. Consciousness like water has a tendency to free itself from the mod of mental system, however, the mod resists and maintain the water and does not let go of the water. Similarly, the mental system tries to maintain the consciousness within itself and does not let go of it. Thus, for consciousness penetrating into our mental system is easy but getting out of it is a major struggle. The excitement, resistance, and distraction, and diversion technics of our mental self, delays the process of becoming free from the trap of mental system. In order to facilitate the process of getting out of mental system, we have obligation to be observant of our negative characteristics, traits, and behavior, recognize our deficiencies which helps us to eliminate and throw away those negative traits.

The main essence of human being is consciousness which not only creates human beings but also human brain and mind through which consciousness becomes aware of itself. When consciousness penetrates into our mental system and physical body, it becomes co-identified and attached to three types of forms: The first form is a structure or network of old thought, belief, opinion, excitement, customs, rites, ceremonies and superstition held by our predecessors that we inherited. These are all mental concepts and also include our roles, positions, power, prestige, social status and job, etc. The second types of forms are excitements and emotions that are under the influence of our thought processes, and include all forms of pains such as emotional pains and sufferings. The third types of forms are our physical body and material things of the external world. As humans when we get attached to these forms or get involved with the affairs of this world, we should not pay one hundred percent of our attention to the worldly things or be drowned in them like children who become involved with their childish games.

The main universal constitution of human is to be parallel and in line with the life of this moment and following this constitution positively affects all our human affairs. Human is nothing but joy and happiness and life plays the musical note of joy for human and produces the vibration of love within human forcing him to dance parallel with the dance of the universe. Life through vibration of our heart, circulate blood through all parts of our body and revitalize our whole system. It is this universal vibration of consciousness that motivates and mobilizes everything in the universe. God or consciousness which is our beloved expresses itself by the lovers, the human beings. It is our love of the beloved which makes the whole world particularly our mental self, which is the center of all negative excitement, envy the universal consciousness. Thus, human responsibility is to re-vibrate the living power and energy of love, joy and tranquility and send it through the world to all other creatures. Human's responsibility, is getting united by the living life of this moment and live at present. Human is not a goal in the future. We need the life of this moment and the events of this moment to join the universal consciousness and this make it possible for us to join the source at any moment.

Being the same as consciousness we would be a productive, positive and creative being, but within our mental system, we turn into evil.

We should be aware that our consciousness is available and with us at all times. Always at this moment a message comes from our consciousness to wake up us from the sleep of mental self, which we should consider and pay attention. We should never leave the living life of this moment and go after the perishable material world. Anything that separates us from our living life of this moment takes us to the past and the future and is useless and harmful to us. Thus, it would be harmful for us to make our mental system active and to live within a space full of pain and sufferings. We are a living life. We do not happen as a living life. Only incidents and events happen and we don't need to show any reaction to these events. We could reach to the state of unlimited space if we do not quarrel with mental system and struggle with it. If we try to stay in the realm of consciousness and unity, the main thing we experience is joy and tranquility. To become depressed or sad, it takes a lot of energy, while to be joyful we don't need that much energy. All we need is to decide to be happy.

Rumi uses many analogies to teach us the laws of life and acceptance of reality as it is. A good analogy between the mental self and our real self or consciousness is the silk worm that behaves based on instinct and eat more and more until becomes so fat that and pregnant to the point that it burst and a butterfly is born with the ability to fly out of carcass of the worm. Butterfly is more free and able to fly and go around and seat on the flowers and drinks the juice of the flowers. When butterfly was in the womb of the worm, did not have a clue that there was a different world out there and world appeared as a limited space. Another analogy is the chick within the egg not being aware of the external world, but through instinct uses the peak to break the egg and become free and jump out of the egg. A person, who has real knowledge and wisdom based on consciousness, is creative and reflects and radiates the positive life giving light to all other people around him/her. This person is already at the presence of universal consciousness and separated from the limited and deficient mental system.

Rumi compares all humans with "Mary" who was pregnant with "Jesus," or "Messiah," the great consciousness and bored the pain of pregnancy and the child birth like any other woman who has to go through the same pain. Similarly, all human beings also have to bear the pain of being pregnant with consciousness, but child birth does not occur without our mental self to go through all the pain and sufferings and reach to the point of giving birth to the consciousness out of the womb of mental system. Even Jesus or Messiah did not lessened, the pain and suffering of Mary during her pregnancy and child birth. Freedom is not possible without struggle, feeling excessive pain and sacrifice. We as consciousness can't be free without sacrificing our mental system. The same way Abraham tried to sacrifice his son the dearest person in his life and a lamb took the place of Ismail as stories in the bible and Quran explained. The sacrificing part of his existence, Abraham really sacrificed his mental self a symbolic action.

According to Rumi, we have two major choices in life: Choice number one, is to flow like water prostrating in the stream rushing down the river toward the sea or ocean of the beloved universal consciousness by acceptance of the life of this moment, not showing any resistance and without fighting or swimming against the flow of water. Thus, we should leave behind our miserable situation within the mental system, and drink the cups of vines of life to experience the new living and loving life. The choice number two is to remain in the dark and cold prison of mental system with all the related pains and sufferings. But even taking the second choice, we could not remain in the mental system for long, because, the universal consciousness lets our internal evil or mental self to cause so much pain and sufferings that we would willingly give up and free ourselves from the prison of mental system.

Universal Consciousness as God and World of Unity as Paradise: A source of Joy and Happiness

Rumi considers God as universal consciousness that exists in all forms in the universe and is the essence of everything in the universe. Consciousness is common denominator of all things and that is the unifying factor. Descartes have similar idea and asserts that "I cannot think of anything but God himself to whose essence belong existence; next, because I cannot understand two or more Gods of this kind; because, having asserted that one God now exist, I plainly see that it is necessarily the case that he has existed from eternity and will endure forever; finally, because I perceive many other things in God, none of which I can remove or change." (Descartes,1979, P. 43). Rumi talks about consciousness and call it different names such as "Pari" or angel, angelic soul, spirit, life, real self, objective self, energy, light, origin, source, etc. Rumi tries not to call it God because as soon as we use a label we have to use our mental system and then, we are talking about a mental God within our mental system not the real objective consciousness. He says we should feel God in ourselves not to use our mental system to construct and know a mental God.

The life of this moment is the most important thing that we can be aware of. But while for some people the life of this moment is paradise, productivity, prosperity, joy and tranquility, for others it may be hell fire, negative thought and destructive excitement. It is at this moment that events can occur and our responsibility in dealing with those events is not to show any reaction, accept the event as it happens, not to judge and not to resist or fight against it. It is the nature of mental self to show reaction particularly negative reaction to any incident no matter if it is perceived as positive or as negative incident or event. We should not let patience which is a virtue turn into waiting which is pain and suffering. Waiting relates to living in the future and being in the prison of time which does not help us but it only creates anxiety and worries. Plants and animal are flexible and patient witnessing the events without any major reaction, thus are relaxing and calm. But mental self within mental system creates reaction for human beings and causes all types of pains. To act like plants and animals in terms of their patience, calmness, flexibility and adaptability helps us to be strong and stable.

VII

Mental Self and Artificial Love

"Dear heart, you are so unreasonable! First you fall in love then worry about your life. You rub and steal then worry about the law. You profess to be in love and still worry about what people say." (Rumi, 13th Century) (Translated from Persian into English by: Mafi & Kolin, 1999, P.75)

The social relationship for a mental self is based on an unequal exchange. Mental self likes to have social relationships with other people however the relationship is based on certain conditions and what mental self can gain from the relationship and from other people. It is through the social relationships that mental self is able to compare self with others, to fight with others, and to create conflict with others. Mental self does not like to compromise, but to control others the way will suite him/her. The social relationship between a mental self and other mental selves is asymmetrical and one way, because mental self wants to know what other people can do for him/her, but does not want to do anything for them. The social relationship of mental self with other mental selves is parasitic and symbiotic and is based on exploitation of other people. Since narcissism is one of major characteristic of mental self, then, mental self considers self the center of the universe and everything and everybody should revolve around him/her. Mental self, evaluates other people in relation to him or herself, based on what type of benefits he/she may receive from them.

Mental self always search for people who have something in common with self. Mental self always compare self with others. If he/she thinks he/she has more knowledge, looks better, has more wealth, higher in his/her position, job or social status, then he/she also obtains a high level of grandiosity. However, if mental self thinks he/she is lower than others in any areas of life, he/she would feel down, depressed, ashamed with low level of self-concept, self-image, and self- identity. It is very hard for mental self to be recognized and feel important without having other mental selves to accept, to pay attention and to confirm his/her artificial existence and falsified greatness. Based on the law of attraction, each person tries to associate with other people who have something in common with the person. If the person has deviant tendencies will be attracted to other people with the same tendencies and if the person is descent and gentle, he/she will search and associate with people of the same sort. Mental self falls in love but it is a mental self, falling in love with a mental picture of another mental self. When people are young they fall in love to the mental picture of another person. But for to people to really fall in love they need to reach to a certain level of maturity of their consciousness and be present at the realm of unity and spiritually love each other not being in love with their physical appearances.

A general understanding of people is that when we get married we will experience happiness. However, this may not be the case. Two individuals who are married will treat each other as mental selves, each one expect the other one to make him/her happy and satisfied. However, the happiness is not in the marriage but within each individual's universal consciousness. Because, as mental systems and mental selves who are center of evil and pain and suffering they only create more pain for each other as long as they are utilizing their mental self but not their real original and objective self. Mental self may think that by getting married or having a relationship, he/she may become more complete, but being deficient to begin with, the mental self, causes more conflict and pain in his/her social relationship. When two mental selves fall in love with each other, their relationship may seem very serious, but it is artificial and temporary and their relationship may dissolve with any minor dissatisfaction or unmet expectation. But two people with real self and consciousness of presence will fall in love and their love is an extension of their love toward the same universal consciousness and the relationship would be a long lasting relationship.

Many inappropriate patterns of mental self, emerges during the marriage of two couples and create major disturbances in their marriage relationship. The main patterns are pattern of resistance, pattern of rage, anger, and violence, pattern of comparing, pattern of criticizing, fault finding and conflict, pattern of high level of expectations, approval and respect which if not met, causes hard feeling, pattern of distrustfulness, pattern of disloyalty, and a pattern of dissatisfaction and conflict and pattern of a sense of insecurity between the couples. Mental self is very pretentious in all his/her relationships. For example mental self may try to look down to earth but within this artificial act and pretense, one can observe the hidden grandiosity and wrong pride within his/her role playing game. If anything does not go according to mental self's expectation, suddenly the artificial pleasantness and pretense turns into anger and rage. Marriage is not just a social relationship or physical attraction between two peoples. It is physical, social, emotional and spiritual bonding between the two couples. Through marriage two couples reach to a higher level of unity.

The unification of two couples is unification of consciousness within two humans. It is not just physical attraction, or sexual desire but also eternal unity between two peoples. Similar physical sexual attraction may occur between a man and a woman. But this type of attraction without marriage is only passion and sexual needs of the individuals without any real bonding and the relationship is only temporary and short lived. However, through marriage a new form of long lasting bond and relationship will emerge and through the marriage the survival of human species becomes possible. A man and woman as husband and wife have their bonding, but after they reproduce their children they become parents with extra thread of bonding because they also receive a new role of parenthood. Combination of parents and children creates the smallest unit of society and the family is considered as an institution or organization.

Thus real love between two people is the love and attraction of consciousness from one person to another person and it is the real love that makes marriage a long lasting phenomenon. A human who is really in love through his/her consciousness would experience joy and happiness in his/her life.

Rumi believes that two different sexes who get married have complementary physical, emotional, psychological, mental and spiritual characteristics which are different from each other. Each couple is considered insufficient and deficient as related to their mental system and mental self. But since the real marriage is for consciousness in two bodies achieving oneness, the husband and wife will experience the unity of the consciousness. Each human being is created with his/her unique beauty and charm and the real beauty comes out of varieties not similarities. Thus, each person has his/her own particular beauty which attracts the other person. But the real beauty is what is inside a person in their spirituality and consciousness which can't be seen but can be felt. The internal beauty is more important than the external beauty. However, a person who has both would be happier. Be aware that we do not own our family members or relatives or even non-relatives. All human being are independent and no one owns anyone else. Thus do not try to force them to accept your old thoughts, beliefs, opinions and excitements. Our children have their own universal consciousness which need to experience the world through them not us.

A man and a woman, who gets married, are not each other's enemy. Their enemy is their mental self which causes problems for both. Consciousness resides in both men and women and as consciousness both group experience the same consciousness and are one within different bodies. But both men and women are whining and crying and complaining and have conflicts with each other which is the relationships of their mental selves. The structure of mental self is like a spider with a deficient web of thought, belief and excitement that can be destroyed easily.

Mental self also falls in love, but the nature of love in this case is more based on passion and interest in physical beauty of the other mate. There is no deep and real love involved in the relationship between two mental selves who are under the influence of their temporary excitement. This type of relationship is a big mistake because it does not last long. Our relationship with life is in a way that we should accept our mistakes and shortcomings and be aware of our attachments to perishable things. Recognizing that we have made mistake can help us not to make the same mistake again but also encourages us to apologize and pay a compensation for those mistakes. If our mistake causes conflict between us and others, then, apology and paying compensation could create peace between us and other people. This condition not only exists between two individuals but also exist between two groups, nations or society. Each human gives the same value and importance to other people which he/she gives to him/herself. Thus if we don't like ourselves and respect ourselves, we can't like or respect others. We only generalize our own characteristics to other people.

When two people with rigid mental self, becomes interested to each other and they may call it love, they may only think of their selfish interests either sexual, monetary or social needs and each may have high level of expectation from the other partner which may not be achievable. If the level of expectation on either side is too high, the other side may not be able to satisfy the level of expectation of his/her mate. That is when problems in their relationship may begin. Due to excessive desires of some mental selves to gain different types of privileges, if one side is not able to provide it, the other side begins to complain and argument starts and may continue for several days. Usually the relationship between two mental selves is based on unequal exchange and it is possible that one side expect more than the other side. This can create conflict in their relationship.

Mental self may become involved with romantic love but the only thing that is romantic in this case is some fantasies and may be some intense longing about the beloved not based on real love but a sense of ownership of the beloved makes the mental self to get excited. Mental self, concentrate on what type of reward or benefit he/she can obtain from the loved one. Love interaction for mental selves is at superficial level even if it may look like a romantic love. Mental selves love is based on being obsessed with the loved one and is in a hurry to get involved with a relationship without giving it enough time to analyze the relationship and the degree of match between the lover and the loved one. Mental self, consider his/her mate as a possession and this sense of ownership leads to control and power tactics which is troublesome. The sense of ownership and being possessive of the loved one create a major sense of irrational jealousy in the lover and damages the love relationship between the couples.

The dysfunctional nature of mental selves love relationship, with a sense of possessiveness, jealousy and control create a major distance between the two couples and creates a constant fear of separation and loss of the loved one. Mental self is not able to tolerate the loss of the loved one and if it happens, goes into a major depression. Mental self, living in psychological time of the past and future and forgetting about the life of this moment causes negative excitements. Thinking about future and the fear of losing loved one create anxieties and worries and living in the past and remembering the negative clashes he/she had with partner makes him/her depressed. Problem is with the nature of mental self which loves to quarrel and fight with someone including his/her mate. Since mental self is not at peace with self can't be at peace with other people. At first when the relationship is brand new, mental self tries to impress his/her partner by putting a mask and show self under positive light.

Mental selves are careful not to disclose information about self but wish to have more information about their partner but usually there would not be mutual self, disclosure because one or both sides try to leave the mask on and play roles and impress each other. But as the intimacy is extended to a higher level and partners disclose more information about selves they begin having problem with each other's perceived deficiencies and shortcomings. At this point the masks are taken off and the real negative traits come to the surface. As soon as mental selves find flaws in each other they could not tolerate, becoming disappointed, hold grudges and a major conflict begins. Mental self is self-centered and sometimes narcissist seeking attention and affection from the partner, but does not feel any obligation to reciprocate the attention or affection. Thus, for mental self it is not a real love that exist between the couples but it is infatuation and physical sexual attraction that bring the couples together.

As couples become more intimate and experience the mutual self-disclosure if it is mutual, then, their real traits and characteristics becomes evident, conflict emerges and they would realize that they are not really match with each other. Part of the problem should be explored within each mental self. If mental self does not have a peaceful and positive relationship with self and does not have self-confident, self-respect, and self-appreciation, then, he/she generalizes the same characteristics to his/her partner and their relationship becomes disrespectful and dysfunctional. In addition to not having self-respect, a mental self, try to determine the life style of his/her partner based on his/her personal needs without paying attention to the other person's need. Mental self also has other major cognitive distortions such as resentment, hypersensitivity, lack of trust and a sense of disloyalty that causes major conflict between the couples and may lead to separation and dissolving their marriage.

Rumi talks about a story of a person who was old and his beard had black and white hairs. He was about to get married and was trying to impress his future wife by showing off that he was still young. Thus, he went to a hair stylist and asked him to remove all the white hairs. He liked to look younger. The hair stylist did cut the man's beard, and put them on the table and told him now, you separate the white hairs from the black ones and he left. Rumi tries to show that the man with white and black beard was trying to go against the process of aging and the evolution of human physical system and did not want to accept the reality of his existence trying to engage in deception. The hair stylist here is a symbol of the consciousness, trying to stop the man from cheating, dishonesty and deceiving his future wife.

Concept of Mental Self as Evil and Mental System as Hell: A Source of Sadness and Depression

Rumi's emphasize on the pain producing tendency and continuous suffering of mental self within the mental system. After part of our universal consciousness becomes separated from its source and penetrates into our mental system, our mental self, causes so much pain for us to get tired of it and try to get out of the hell of mental system. Mental self with its pain producing, pain addicting and evil tendency, produces, many forms of mental, psychological and physical diseases and discomfort in humans. This idea is also reflected in Peck's statement that "This tendency to avoid problems and the emotional suffering inherent in them is the primary basis of all human mental illness. Since most of us have this tendency to a greater or lesser degree, most of us are mentally ill to a greater or lesser degree, lacking complete mental health." (Peck1978, P.17). The chronic sadness and depression is caused by our mental self that is confused and at war with self, creating a major internal conflict. In order for human to really escape the internal conflict is to shut down the mental system and try to be at peace with self. Only after being in peace with ourselves we will be able to have peace with other people.

The concept of "mental self", ego or evil by Rumi is equivalent of the concept of "necrophilia" a true love of death by Fromm, and the Concept of "real, objective self or consciousness", a true joy, happiness, tranquility and creativity by Rumi, is equivalent of "biophilia", a true love of life by Fromm. Fromm stated that "The person with necrophilious orientation is one who is attracted to and fascinated by all that is not alive, all that is dead; corpses, decay, feces, dirt… The opposite of the necrophilious orientation is the biophillious; its essence is love of life in contrast to love of death… (Fromm1964, P. 38) He elaborated on "Biophilia", in his books "For the love of life" (Fromm, 1983) and "The Art of Loving." (Fromm, 1956). Human is either mental self with physical mental consciousness which is an artificial and distorted reflection of universal consciousness or a combination of both consciousness or mental self at any moment. Our origin has been with us from the beginning of our existence in different forms and at different stage of our evolution, thus, we have never been really separated from our origin but while within the forms, we have been unaware during the time that we resided in different forms and even within our mental system.

Within Mental system we are not our real self, we are only a label, a name, and a role that other people put on us to artificially identify us and we are so attached to material things that those things becomes our identification and without them we think that are nothing. Rumi advices us to listen to the trumpet of life, joy and tranquility which gives us the message of freedom and independence from the bondage of attachment to the worldly things. The mental self creates and intensify the pain because it is made of pain and suffering. The negative excitement of our mental self, prevent us from reaching the treasure of presence which is being at presence of universal consciousness. To express our love is to experience the joy and happiness and radiating it to all other people around us. Life expresses itself through us. Thus we and God are the same. We become one with consciousness and the consciousness provides abundance to the world through us. We should get out of the physical mental consciousness of mental self and become intoxicated by love of consciousness. Within mental system life becomes entrapped and we can't live. Life need to be lived not to be saved. Unlived life isn't life.

Mental system as a center of hell and mental self as evil can only produce pain and sufferings. If we stay within our mental system, we will feel alone even if we are within a big group of people. The reason for the hearts that are sad and don't experience the happiness is that mental self, doesn't want to be happy. Our main mistake and sin is that we separated ourselves from our source and experienced the bitter taste of the vine of mental self and our life has been stolen from us. Before our sadness intensifies and our emotional and psychological pains affect our physical body and paralyze our reason, it is better to get out of the dark prison of mental system and experience the sweet vine of life and joy of rejoining our consciousness. Life is in abundance and never really ends, thus, we should consume it to the max and not try to save it. To become attached to this world increases the roots of sadness and extends many sub-roots of pains. Thus, we should cut the root of sadness and depression before it grows even further.

To Rumi Mental system is the hell within human beings where all the major physical, mental and psychological pain and sufferings occurs. The agent of mental system or hell is the evil of mental self that only creates pain and suffering through negative thoughts, beliefs, opinions, customs, rites, excitements, emotions. Mental self is the artificial being as evil which works through duality of opposites and like to have other mental selves to fight with. Mental system and mental self, combined also have tendency to engage in the evil practice of idol worshipping that all religion without exception forbid this practice. All the old civilization and people who engaged in idol worshipping and became co-identified and attached to the idols such as gold, silver, money, luxury, and even other humans went astray and became slave of those idols instead of paying attention and becoming aware of their own internal treasure of consciousness within themselves. This process of worshipping idols went so far as to the extreme limit that people even worship imaginary, hallucinatory and visionary mental concepts including mental God or worshipping the false human idols such as the concept of "American Idol," which presents a temporary perishable beauty forgetting that the same idol or beautiful girl will become an ugly person when she gets old. This type of idol worshipping is very similar to the "Golden cow" that was made by "Samari" in the Sinai desert. All these are symbols of attachment, co-identification and codependency to the material world.

We as human beings using our mental system and mental self as an agent of evil have been co-identified and attached to our own thought and beliefs that we become obsessive in emphasizing and defending them. We have become highly confused under the magical spell of our own distorted thought and beliefs and constantly compare our own beliefs with others to find a deficiency in them and try to put them down. This comparison also occurs as related to our material belongings when we want to know if others have more or less than us and then use it to judge other people based on what they have or what they do not have. This sense of comparison is a pain producing addiction and obsession a disease of our mind and mental system. To become co-identified by other human beings even with our family members we lose our freedom and take their freedom from them. This will create a group of co-identified and co-dependent people who are not independent and will not be able to take care of their own life by themselves. The solution is not to become co-identified with anyone or anything, instead to concentrate on the love, equality, being non-judgmental and joy and happiness.

Mental self always engages in perseverative, continuous and repetitive thought process. However most of mental self's thought content is negative and based on cognitive distortion or erroneous thinking patterns. Examples are: wrong conception of time, suspicious of others, distrustful, a sense of being incomplete, an excessive need to get attention. Need to control others, etc. To Rumi, Demons, and angels are only our mental constructs and we see all beauties as angels and all ugliness as demons. This is based on the duality of our mental system and mental self. The only demon is our mental self and the only angel is our consciousness which is the real beauty and essence of human beings. The more active our mental self becomes, the more chains of old thoughts, beliefs, opinions, attitudes, and excitements go through our mind and mental system. This is the main source of our distraction and lack of concentration on major issues in our daily life. Peck (1983) also believed that "Satan cannot do evil except through a human body... the only power that Satan has is through human belief in its lies... This book is entitled "People of the Lie" because lying is both a cause and a manifestation of evil." (Peck PP. 206, 242). Peck's Concept of the "People of the lie," is equivalent of the concept of "mental self" by Rumi. As Rumi explains the mental system is the center of evil and the mental self is the representative of evil within our mental system.

Rumi uses example of the story of Solomon and his ring and power of understanding animals and talking to them as the power of consciousness. He believes that the consciousness of Solomon, exist within every human being and this consciousness makes us aware of both, seen or material world and unseen or spiritual world. The demon or mental self always try to steal the Solomon ring of consciousness and gives us back the physical mental consciousness within the mental system so that we can create a relationship with our natural environment and experience the external world through our mental system and mental self. Our consciousness provides us with the power of recognizing our shortcomings and the limitation of our mental system. Rumi uses many important historical religious people who positively influence human society as representatives of consciousness of presence including Abraham, Joseph, Jacob, Khizr, Zoroaster, Solomon, Moses, Jesus, Buddha, Mohammad to name a few. He also uses historical figures who were representative of evil, demon and mental self, such as Pharaohs, Nimrod, etc.

We as human beings are trapped within dark atmosphere of our mental system. We have become bitter, drowsy and sluggish and we are getting tired of this miserable life that our mental system has created for us. We have chosen the wrong route, marching in the dark and need to find the right way which is letting life lead us to the bright light of the morning when we feel the presence. We are joy of life and like flowers we are aware of our beauty and preciousness. Our main music is the sound of drum and flute of joy that is our prayer. The sound of cheerful music of life should be played in all particles of our existence and that is our prayer because the universal consciousness spread the joy through humans to all part of the universe. Rumi says the only force that could put off the elevated fire of mental self, is power of love of consciousness. Rumi addresses the wine distributer to stop giving him the wine of events and mental self that is not suitable for him and asks the distributer of the wine of life to give him the life giving wine of annihilation.

God or consciousness has created life as forms and penetrated into forms to experience life. But human mental self, destroys life individually under the influence of its anger, rage and vengefulness and destroy the life of millions of human beings, animals and plants though wars and creation of destructive bombs including the nuclear and hydrogen bombs. Thus if we let our mental self as the representative of evil to take over, humanity and human civilization as we know it today will perish and vanish through biological, chemical and nuclear wars or other forms of mass destructive powers. Our mental self is very ugly inside, but tries to show that it is beautiful from outside. The constant pain and suffering that mental self creates for self and others can't be hidden even though mental self always has a mask on and hides its ugly face under the mask. This mask appears as soon as our consciousness unconsciously goes into the mental system and creates the temporary artificial physical and mental self. But due to the main nature of mental self that is inducing pain and suffering, the physical and mental consciousness has to free itself from the hell of mental system.

Evil is a distorted being that is made of three major mental forms: The first is excitement form or emotions, the second is thought form, and the third is mental form. Mental self is the representative of evil within the pain producing space of hell or mental system. Hell is the space of negative energy. Evil is a complementary part of each human and lives within each human, serving the function of producing excessive pain so that we would try to get out of our internal hell or mental system and dissolve our mental self. If there would not be any human, there would not be any evil. In order to dissolve our mental self, we should stop engaging in negative thoughts and negative excitement such as cognitive distortions, negative emotions such as sadness, depression, anger, greed, complaining and superstitious beliefs.

One form of evil is the way we look at other people with pain and rage. The evil eyes are the eyes of mental self that has destructive power and hypnotizes other people with negative energy and create reaction and negative excitements in other mental selves and makes them physically, mentally, and emotionally sick. Evil eyes' energy can't penetrate through the eyes of people who already experienced the positive power of universal consciousness and reached to the treasure of presence. The eyes of mental self are the eyes of fault finder and constricted eyes which only see negativity and defect. Evil eyes are eyes of the hidden enemy within us which constantly create pain and suffering for us while pretending to be our friend, gives beautiful emotional speeches, but sings the songs of war play the drum of war and finds many excuses to start a war with imaginary and artificially perceived enemies. While the thorns will provide beautiful flowers as their fruit of consciousness, the mental self produces ugly and dried branches of pains and sufferings. A good test of being aware of our evil mental self is to see if we do not feel joy when other people are joyful and happy, or when we are joyful when other people are sad and unhappy.

VIII

Different Dimensions of Mental Self Physical, Social, Spiritual, Personality and Religious Dimensions of Mental Self

*"Peaceful is the one who's not concerned with having more
or less. Unbounded by name and fame he is free from sorrow
from the world and mostly from himself (Rumi, 13th Century)
Translated from Persian into English by Mafi & Kolin
(1999, p. 35)."*

Human beings have many dimensions and all these dimensions are in the process of constant change and evolution. Human physical dimension or self is constantly renews itself and all types of human cells are dying and rejuvenating as time passes. Human mental dimension or self is also in a state of constant change. Not only all the information and data are being restored in human mind or mental system based on the data or information received through our senses and nervous system, but also all these information and data will be analyzed and modified constantly based on our continuous experiences. Individual's social self also is in a constant state of change based on social events or situations we experience. Our religious dimension also changes based on our experiences. Our spiritual dimension changes throughout our life and we become more spiritual and transcendental when we become more mature and older.

Physical Dimension of Mental Self

Rumi considers the physical dimension of self a horizontal dimension which includes our body as a physical biological system and mental system. Our awareness of our physical system is based on two different types of experiences:

1. Physical Experience. We become aware of our body through our senses and nervous system and have a direct contact with our environment. Our senses helps us to experience the external world and our immediate environments through auditory, hearing, olfactory, smelling, visual, seeing, touching, tasting and receiving motion sensory stimulation, we become aware of everything within our environment. These are our sense experience.

2. Mental experience. In addition to our direct physical contact with our environment, we also have a mental relationship with our environment which is based on how we mentally perceive our environment and our contact with the environment. It is very important for us to have a match between our physical experience and mental experience of our environment. If these two experiences are parallel with each other and match each other, we can make sense of our external physical reality. However, if the physical experience does not match with our mental experience, we will not be able to make a sense of external physical environment and we become mentally confused and sick.

Rumi believes that our mental experience is biased due to deficiency of our mental system and mental self that see the world through dark and polluted glasses. Rumi believes that the relationship between Physical body and thought within human physical system is the relationship between two realms of energy at two different levels. These two realms of energy are an extension of the universal consciousness in the body's form of energy. All different forms from solids, going through plants, animals and finally human being are universal consciousness in concentrated forms of energy. What unites all the particles of the universe and attract them toward each other is not the gravity, but it is the universal consciousness in the form of electrical vibration and chemical impulses. The physical self needs to be harmonized with the continuous dance of all forms and parts of the universe through "Sama" or a twirling dance of the dervishes which symbolizes the dance of all germs and different parts of the universe.

According to Rumi, human body has the basic needs of air, water and food and movement and rest or sleep to survive, however, we eat to stay alive but we are not living to eat. Along with basic physical needs, we also have the preservation instinct to help us to stay safe and secure our life. Movement is very important because every germ and part of the universe is alive and needs movement. Human body being as one of the live organism has been created to move and adapt to its social physical environment. Consciousness penetrates the fetus in our mother's womb during her pregnancy period and is with us for the rest of our life until our physical body and mental system dies or transfers to different forms of energy and then goes back and rejoins our origin. All human have a tendency to reach to security, freedom, independence, relax-ation and comfort in their life and without it they can't stay normal. Maslow, stated that " To summarize briefly, the loss of the basic-need satisfactions of safety and protection, belongingness, love, respect, self-esteem, identity, and self- actualization produces illnesses and deficiency diseases. " (1971, p. 22).

Our body is a multiple system made of the physical/biological, mental and excitement system. The physical body is not just physical. It has another dimension which is the etheric body, angelic soul or real self or conscious-ness and energy which create motion in our whole body. The etheric body or angelic soul is the boundary between our physical system and the external world. Our consciousness being eternal teaches us that our physical mental system is perishable and temporary system and could not exist forever. Our original consciousness is being absorbed by our mental system like a sponge. The consciousness trapped within our mental system, establishes the mental self which in turn creates negative thought, emotions and excitements which causes our pains and suffering. Rumi believes that we do not have a choice but to be under this type of pain and suffering which in the long run has a positive function and forces us to free ourselves out of the mental system. Our observing universal consciousness is observing our physical and mental consciousness trapped within our mental system and observes the deviant actions of our mental selves.

The physical, psychological and emotional pains and suffering intensifies whenever we decide to pull away from our attachments and co-identifications with the material and non-material items we have been attached with. We can jump out of mental system through a small space of light leading to the source of light. The small space is the life of this moment. All the interactions among people is through their mental selves or egos which is artificial distorted and transitory. We should feel all the pains and suffering consciously and decide to jump out of our mental system when the time is ripe. Our trapped consciousness is like a bird waiting to fly out of our mental system but this will happen when we are no longer able to bear the intensified pain and suffering. Thus, we have no choice but to free ourselves out of the bondage of our mental system. Rumi put a lot of emphasis on change as the law of life and believes that all our dimensions are in a constant state of change and at any new moment we are a newly revised person within all our dimensions including physical, emotional, psychological and spiritual. Rumi advices human to accept any change and do not react or resist against it negatively, because as we grow older, we lose a lot of skills, abilities and concentration. It is the nature of the evolution of consciousness that our body, mental system and mental self will all perish to let consciousness to go free.

We possess senses within our physical, biological and nervous systems, which help us to hear the sound, observe the sceneries, smell the fragrances, taste the foods and touch and feel the environmental things. There is a reason that we have all these senses. Our senses help us to become aware of our physical and social environment and relate to everything outside our body. Each sense provides us with a unique way of experiencing the external world. What would be the value of natural sounds of nature, the voices of birds and animals and the sound of the wind blowing through the trees and mountains and valleys as well as singings of other human beings and their musical instruments without having human ears to listen to those voices and sounds? What would be the value of all the beautiful creatures including other human beings and the beauty of the different sceneries of the mountains, valleys, trees, lakes, seas, oceans, the blue sky and the sun during the day and with all the planets and stars and the moon during the night, the green fields and the beautiful flowers if we did not have eyes to see them?

Similarly, what would be the value of all the rejuvenating fragrances of flowers, plants, herbs and other nice smelling materials in the world, if we did not have a sense of smell? Without a sense of smell we could not even distinguish between the nice smell, and something that would have a bad smell. Imagine how could we taste all the good edibles and foods without a sense of taste? It would be a boring life for us if we would not have a sense of touch both physically and sexually. All these senses are adapted to different aspects of our environment so that we as human could experience the external world and enjoy life. This is another reason why human being is the special being that the whole universe is in a constant dance of life to please the human beings.

Human brain is the highest level of evolution of the material form and the human consciousness is the highest level of evolution of the human mind. The whole universe on the surface appears to be solid and is presented as forms, but deep down every particles of universe in its smaller part is nothing but consciousness and light in energy form. The solids look like stable and motionless, however, everything within the smallest parts of things are in a constant and rapid motion. All the forms are transitory and change from one form to the other. But consciousness always is formless, timeless, and eternal. Thus, everything in the universe is made of realms of energy and consciousness. All humans who try to go against the flow of the universal consciousness, or try to go through the wrong path either reach a dead end or will perish. Young mental selves thinking that they have a long life of this world ahead of them, try to live in the future which is only a mental construct. The old mental selves thinking that they are getting close to the end of their worldly life try to live in the past and remember the good old days which, is a mental construct and a picture in their mind. The people who experienced a high level of consciousness live at present and enjoy the life of this moment.

Rumi uses the watermill and the river as an example to show the dynamic state of life. The water of the river, hits the boards on the water mill and fills the containers that are attached to the boards and while the power of the water pushes the boards down, the wheel of water mill starts revolving around its shaft which is attached to a second shaft and by turning the second shaft it also turns a huge and heavy round stone that moves in circle over another stone and grinds the wheat or other types of seeds and turns the seeds into flour, which then will be turned into paste of flour and finally cooked in the oven as bread. Then, the bread maker sells the bread and makes money to support his family life and pays for his daily expenses. This is an example of dynamic state and flow of life within all things. The same way that without water, the watermill could not work, the same way, we can't live without water of life.

A human who is alive with presence and experience a high level of consciousness within is able to have a creative mind and thought and provides productive knowledge and wisdom to others. But, a person with a rigid mental self has only physical and mental consciousness which is limited and deficient, thus, produces a line of negative and deviant thought which is destructive. A visionary thinker instead of being alive with the life of this moment spends his/her time thinking about the future and death. This type of mental self has distorted thinking and is imprisoned within the mental system.

Social Dimension of Mental Self and Society

Rumi believes that our social self is under the influence of society or community and that our mental self always intervene and convince us that whatever, group of people or mental selves are doing is right due to the power of the group or collection of mental, social selves. Thus, we copy whatever the group does. The problem arises out of the fact that group of people have their own old belief, thoughts, opinions, and negative excitements and transfer those negative ideas and beliefs to the individual who consider him/herself as social self and part of the group. Mental self can't be recognized or approved without other members of society or group. Thus, has to associate with others but he / she will find someone with common traits. Society controls people and put a lot of stress on our mental self which always resist and fight against any form of stress, however, mental self may reach to the point of satiation and gives up and develops a sense of mental numbness and becomes neutral to his/her social environment.

The social relationship of the mental self is asymmetrical and is based on an unequal exchange meaning that a mental self relates to others based on what other people can do for him/her not what he can do for them. Mental self expects others to comply with whatever he/she dictates and perform according to his/her expectations. Mental self always wants something from others but is not willing to reciprocate and give others anything. However, mental self has to be around people to be able to influence them. Our individual mental self is not the same as our social mental self. Social self is a type of imaginary and artificial self that we develop under the influence of a group, community or society. A social mental self, acts, based on the rules of the group and is not as independent as an individual mental self. People within the group agree on a common criterion or goal and create political, social, economic, religious, sport, or even criminal group. All the members of these different types of groups are co-identified with each other and blindly follow the activities and the rules of the group.

According to Rumi, different people who are raised within the same social environment may develop different types of selves. However their mental selves have something in common all have tendency to produce excitement, and emotional, and psychological pain. Thus the same social environment may produce different types of self, due to human internal traits and the degree of rigidity of mental self. Rumi uses several examples to show different influences of the same social environment on different people. The bees drink the juice of the flowers from the same area and living within the same environment, one produces, honey and the other one poison. Two deer which eat the same plant and drink the same water, one deer produces pure fragrance of musk or scent and the other produces only feces. Another example he gives is the bamboos that may be within the same field and consume the same minerals and water, however, one is full of sugar and the other one is empty inside. Rumi uses an analogy and consider the society of human beings as a pomegranate. All the seeds within the pomegranate look different, but all are part of the same system arranged in a way to complete the whole pomegranate. If we squeeze the pomegranate, we get the same juice from all the seeds.

The main common essence of all human being is consciousness in the state of energy. All human beings have a domain or area of energy within and around them. Einstein stated that "wherever we have a mass we also have energy within it. To him if we divide the energy by the mass what we get is the cosmological constant or consciousness. $C2 = E/M$." Thus, consciousness exists in the form of energy and colorless light that can't be seen by our eyes. Each individual has his/her own energy level but within the group all the energies will influence each other in a geometrical way producing a high level of energy that energizes every individual in the group. This is one of the reason people get together during different ceremonies, parties, and other forms of gatherings to be socialized and energized. The higher level of consciousness can influence lower level of consciousness. Thus people who are at a higher level of consciousness can influence other people who have lower level of consciousness. This may occur through the vibration of energy between the two people or through induction and charging another person similar to the group charging the individual members.

To Rumi, society is more than just human society. He considers all living creatures such as animals, plants, nature including water, clouds, fogs and

non-living like solids part of the society of beings and as the universal consciousness within the forms. He believes that we can't be part of the general
society of all beings through our limited mental system. First we have to
become colorless and formless with tranquility of presence at this moment
to maintain our vibrating essence or soul within our body and feel the joy of
the dance of our soul within us. Since consciousness is within all the general
society's beings and there is only one consciousness in the whole universe,
thus, every part of the universe is in the process of unification and oneness.
In order for us to reach to the unity, we have to become the colorless and
weightless light. Becoming aware of our consciousness helps us to become
more aware of our external world. We are not able to really get out of this
moment at any time to go to the past or to the future. We always stay at
present time. To be at peace with ourselves and others, we have to be able to
resolve our internal conflict between the evil mental system and our etheric
angelic soul or consciousness by concentrating on our consciousness and
deactivating our mental self.

Current human societies are not societies based on love and real support of
their individuals. Individuals in societies have become highly individualized,
divided, separated through many artificial labels such as nationalities, eth-
nicities, races, social and economic classes, privilege classes, political, religious
groups, interest groups, multinational corporations as invisible empires with
branches almost in every society controlling human life and living. Societies
are so individualized and divided that people feel lonely and depressed even
if they live in society and groups. Thus, people try to join different groupings
for a new sense of identity and belongingness. Human being trapped in their
mental system and acting as mental selves is busy creating pains and suffering
for self and others and part of that separation creates sadness and loneliness.
In current human societies, individuals do not have their individual and social
independence and freedom due to two major factors: First, they sacrificed
their social freedom for the sake of security. Second, they lost their individual freedom because they live within their prison or hell of mental system
and instead of being an independent person they are attached, co-identified

and co-dependent with roles, labels, positions, material belongings, religion, nationality, race, ethnicity, thoughts, beliefs, opinions, and excitements.

The social dimension of mental self is also very complicated and disturbing because of many artificial mental concepts or constructs such as reputation, status, position, power and privilege, credibility etc., which entraps people and control their life. When we try to please others, we may not be able to do that all the time. Mental self is always worried and anxious that he/she may lose his/her reputation, and works hard to maintain an artificial reputation. Mental self likes to maintain his/her social, political and economic status but, become embarrassed when he/she loses that. Social, economic, political and bureaucratic positions are other artificial concepts that create a constant fear for mental self not to lose them. Mental self likes to be powerful, however, power is only a transitory mental concept and mental self can lose it at any time. Mental self loves social privileges and likes to maintain it all the time. Credibility is another mental concept and it is very hard for mental self not to have it. The real fear of human perceptually is to show the real nature of their self which is ugly, artificial, transitory and empty. Not having all these artificial concepts that are important for mental self is very painful.

When consciousness is pure it has unlimited depth and roots, but, mental self being artificial shadow, does not have any depth or root. Two couples are the same consciousness within the realm of unity. However, most husbands and wives deal with each other as mental selves and see each other as forms and roles. Mental self is deficient and when two mental selves with major sense of deficiency get married each side thinking that they can eliminate their sense of deficiency through marriage and can become happy in life. But, the sense of deficiency continues even after marriage and may even get worse. Both couples each have their own specific mental selves with all their negative and erroneous thought, belief, opinion and excitement and by getting together there would be clashes between them due to all the negative thought and cognitive distortions. Problem arises from the tendency of each couple with pains to go after someone with similar pains which only ends up to separation and dissolving the marriage. Thus, two couples are complementary with each other as consciousness but contrastive as mental selves.

All humans are the same consciousness and the unity of society comes from the unity of consciousness within all members of the society. The major difference among the members of the society is in their forms only which includes mental systems, physical system, psychological tendencies, personality make ups and emotional characteristics. The members of the society and groups within society are also different in terms of their beliefs, opinions, traditions, ceremonies, and excitements. All the religions of the world appeared to help people to achieve unity, equality, social justice and tried to increase the value of human being as a special and unique being, the master of all existence. However, the main functions of religions changed and deviated from its right path after the prophets and founders of those religions died. Interest groups and people with political, social, economic and religious power and prestige changed the rules and functions of all religions based on their personal or group interests. Today, we see that certain groups, societies, or governments use religion as a tool to create division, separation and conflict among people to make it easy for them to control and take advantage of people. These are individual or group mental selves who benefit from all these conflicts in many different ways.

Spiritual Dimension of Self

All human beings have a spiritual dimension which is the highest level of their existence and is considered the universal consciousness or treasure of presence. As human, we are not able to reach our real spiritual dimension through our deficient and incomplete logic and reason of our mental self. Our senses, nerves, thought, beliefs, opinions and excitement as well as our logic and reason that comes from our mental system and establishes our mental self does not have the power and ability of comprehending our spiritual dimension or the universal consciousness. It is only through an unconditional love that we can become aware of our origin or the universal consciousness. Love, is a vibration within our whole system that connect us and help us to rejoin to our source or origin. It is our spiritual self or consciousness that pulls away and releases our physical and mental consciousness from the bondage of our mental self. Universal consciousness is selfless, formless, timeless and eternal. Rumi considers the spiritual dimension a vertical dimension which is the dimension of this moment, moment of unity, life dimension, eternal, unlimited, formless and timeless. The major motivational force of spiritual dimension is love.

Rumi believes that the spiritual self is searching for a real meaning in life. In the similar vein, Frankl (1998, p.121) stated that the most basic motivation for human is struggle to search for a meaning in life. Frankl stated that people who lose their effort to find a meaning in their life, experience a state of "emptiness of existence". Rumi believes that the main struggle for human being is to find a meaning in his/her life to save them from the pains and excitement that is being created by our mental selves. Real spirituality can only be achieved through love but not logic or reason. According to Rumi, there exist a strong tendency in human that can't relax unless sees him/herself connected with his/her origin and the universal consciousness. Knowing that he/she is connected to the origin of our existence, we strive to return to it. Only being aware of this type of connection we as humans can internally relax and maintain our hope and find a real meaning in our life.

Rumi believes that we have our major senses, which help us to relate to our environment and collect information we need to make a sense of our external world. However, we as human also have a spiritual sense which relates us to the universal consciousness and the eternal, unlimited world of unity. This sense is the consciousness trapped within our mental system and is being used by our mental self. It is through our physical consciousness that we relate to the universal consciousness and experience objective spirituality. Our spiritual self is superior and above our physical, mental and social selves. Universal consciousness penetrates into all forms including human form to experience every aspect and dimension of our existence through us. When we reach to high level of consciousness, we can see without our sensual eyes, we can hear without our sensual ears and we talk without using our tongue or any particular language. Because anything we receive through our physical senses helps our mental system and self to relate to the external world and gives us a sense of identification with different aspects of material world. But, we need to use the unlimited universal language of consciousness.

In order to have a better world we should educate and train more people with the power of spirituality and the divine of presence. Because people with confused mental selves who are sleep within the mental system are not able to create a balanced society. With inadequate, artificial and confused mental system, the mental selves can only create conflict, combativeness and wars among nations and the emerging society would be a chaotic social and physical environment for human beings. The sensory eyes of mental selves can only see the forms or material things, lands, houses, cars, planes, luxuries, and other material belongings such as gold, silver and precious stones not the real value of humanity and spirituality, thus they march in their material world without any opportunity for transcendental advancement. The world of meaning is the world of formlessness, and nothingness and we should always be in contact with the world of meanings through our spiritual senses.

Human can become aware of his/her internal consciousness and use it to suppress the mental system and the mental self. All the prophets who emerged among human beings were those who reached to a high level of spirituality and transcendental elevation and felt the universal consciousness within themselves and tried to lead other people through the right path so that everybody could experience the same type of enlightenment. "The word "Zoroaster" means light of stars (Shahbazi, 2015); the name and the word "Buddha," means "the awakened one," (Ctzen.org.) The Name "Moses" is derived from a Hebrew name "Mosheh" could possibly mean "Deliver," in Hebrew."(Danzinger). It is considered consciousness taken from the water; the word "Jesus" means the resurrected consciousness, and the word

"Mohammad" means the "Praiseworthy,' derived from Arabic word "Hamid meaning "to praise." (Aryan Pur-Kashani, 2004). Human is heritage of the prophets and has the vine of life and consciousness within themselves. Rumi believes that we should be loyal and return to and unite with our universal consciousness. The calming voice of consciousness makes us awaked and the harsh voice of our mental self puts us into sleep which gives us nightmares, pain and suffering.

It is our spiritual dimension that works like a control valve and coordinates all of our other dimensions. Our spiritual dimension brightens the light for us to see and observe our shortcomings within other dimensions. When an event happens and our mental self is not able to understand what has happened, it is our spiritual dimension and the consciousness that intervenes and provides awareness and recognition of the unknown. But our mental self is very hard to stay quiet and tries to intervene without enough knowledge and information. Our realm of unity which is nothingness is not made of sound. Sound is produced within the silent space of unity and dissolves within the silent space. Sound is very temporary but realm of unity is eternal. Thus silence gives birth to sound and then swallows the sound. As consciousness we are negation of all worldly things and all our other dimensions. Without consciousness as energy our physical, emotional and mental system are defective and useless. Why we should get hot with the fever of the fire of our mental self when we are the realm of messiah and the physician of consciousness who cure all pains and sufferings.

To worship God or consciousness means to sense God within and to be aware of the internal sound of consciousness. To pray is being parallel to the life of this moment. Our pray ends when we come out of the life of this moment, we use our mental system which, takes us to the past or future. Mental self is attracted toward external world but, a person who is experiencing the present is attracted to the realm of unity. We continue to search for universal consciousness until we rejoin it. As soon as we become one with our origin the search stops. The real and the best repentance is returning from the mental system and dissolving our mental self. If we use the power of love to rejoin our consciousness and origin then, there is no need for repentance. Love of our origin dissolves the repentance. Love by itself is able to unite us with the universal consciousness. But we do not need to travel or go far to find the consciousness. It is within us and all we need is to become aware of and become one with it. The friend and enemy of God are beings separated from God and have mental selves. We are neither enemy nor friend of God. We are one with God or consciousness within us.

Personality Dimension of Mental Self

Mental self being an artificial, temporary concept and phenomenon with physical mental consciousness learns through his/her life span from parents and other people to play role, impress others, obtain attention and approval of other. Thus, our mental self uses a mask not to show to other people our real face of negativity, deviancy and pain addicting personality of our mental self. Mental self is based on duality and having two opposites fighting each other. Thus, has to have another mental self to compare and to fight with. Without "he/she," mental self can't make his "he" stronger. In order for mental self to be able to fight with another mental self, he/she has to find something in another person that he/she does not approve and is against with. Therefore, the mental self tries to find fault in others, blaming others, putting others down, etc. Thus personality of mental self is based on conflict, contrast and quarrel.

Mental self, has a strong sense of excitements which include: constant fear, anger, rage, paranoia, suspiciousness and distrust toward others as well as anxiety, depression, sadness and worries. Mental self always is afraid that something bad may happen. Thus, mental self can't relax at any time. Mental self loves to cause pain for self and others and through pain and suffering makes self, more important and bigger than normal. However, the same pain producing tendency of the mental self is the main force behind destruction of mental self when the time is right. Since our mental self always think that he/she is not strong enough and is not big enough, has to gather other mental self to look stronger and try to create a bigger conflict at a group level. According to Rumi all the negativity in our thought, beliefs, opinions, excitements, emotions and all our mental and psychological problems relate to the pain producing activities of our mental self. Group mental selves also benefit from each individual mental self, thus, tries to keep all the individuals within the group united and does not let go of the individuals.

The group of individual selves which gains a new artificial identity no matter what type of group organization or institution they belong to, emphasize on the loyalty of each individual mental self and punish each individual self if he/she does not follow the rules or instructions of the group. The group gives each individual mental self, different label such as artificial sense of status, role, position and being important. The leader of the group may try to create bad reputation for any individual mental self who violates the rules of the group and accuse him/her of disloyalty and betrayal. Certain religious groups will ex-communicate their members if the individual mental self does not blindly obey the rules of the group. Thus each group also creates its own group personality which includes all the personality problems that an individual mental self could possess. The problem with being a member of the group is that, people try to join different groups top gain a sense of new identity which is artificial identity. It is possible that the mission of the group is a deviant and criminal, but the member still feel good just to have a sense of new identity even if the group itself is not approved by society at large.

When our false reputation is recognized and approved by others, we feel satisfied and happy, but when our reputation goes under question or endangered, we become threatened, irritable and angry. Reputation is only a mental concept and is artificial. Thus we really don't have a real reputation to lose and we should not take it seriously. What we consider reputation, enthusiasm and chastity are all mental concepts. What we try to hide from people are all our artificial internal traits that we don't want other people to know about. Artificial reputation is nothing but creating pain and suffering for the one who thinks he/she has it. Life does not flow within these artificial concepts.

Our mental self, is made of artificial chastity and existence. To give a sense of existence to material objects and beliefs and to become attached to them and consider them our chastity which is an artificial reputation. We become angry because of our un-satiated appetite and excessive wants or greed for wealth and luxuries and when we internally stuff our anger it turns into vengefulness and remain within our mental system, waiting to explode. In order to stop our internal evil of mental self, we have to forget or throw away our anger, vengefulness, jealousy and greed.

Religious Dimension of Mental Self

Metal self pretends to have a religion and uses mental system to create an artificial mental God and try to worship a mental concept. A group of mental selves create their own mental God based on their group experiences and interaction with the external, social, and physical environment. Then they try to assign God with their human traits and characteristics. The next step is that group with the power of the group which is nothing but the power of each individual combined with the power of every other individual will control each member. The problem emerges when we create an artificial concept through our mental system and make ourselves satisfied and brainwashed that we have to worship the result of our own mental creation. Since the beginning of time when human being emerged, mental selves began to use their mental system to create varieties of gods based on their group experiences thus producing many different varieties of the concepts of God. While there is only one united consciousness or God, mental self and mental selves believe in many Gods because of their distorted mental system.

Through our ancestors, we have been thought to develop a sense of guilt because our first human predecessors, Adam and Eve made a mistake or committed a sin. Since the beginning of human life and developing a history and philosophy of our life, considering that our ancestors made a mistake, we began to pray our mentally constructed God to have mercy on us and forgive us for what we did not have anything to do with. What Adam and Eve did is the same thing that all human being do which is going into their mental system as consciousness and developing mental system and mental self. Then, our mental self becomes attached and co-identified with the worldly materials and our thought, beliefs, and excitement. We don't need to pray and ask for forgiveness because we have not done anything wrong. The only sin and mistake is to get into our mental system, develop a mental self, sleeping within the mental system and becoming attached and co-identified with worldly things. This sense of guilt comes from the artificial, distorted and transitory mental self which is the center of all pains and sufferings and this is one way for mental self to protect and maintain self. Self-blame is a major characteristic of mental self. In most people the realm of unity has been closed and only their mental self is operating. Rumi says why we should be afraid of a needle when we have the cutting sword of consciousness within our reach.

What becomes a real problem is for mental selves to cling on their artificial religion and become co-identified and attached to the artificial mental concept of God that they have created themselves. While God is nothingness, formless, timeless, unlimited, eternal consciousness which is within everything in the universe including within human beings, then why we are looking for God somewhere else. The main acting agent within us which controls our body and mental system is consciousness not the mental self. Thus, human being is the best manifestation of God or consciousness, light and energy. Our responsibility as human is that we should let God or consciousness within us to work through us to help us becoming one with God or consciousness. For those mental selves that create an artificial and distorted concept of God in their mental system and try to ask that mental concept to help them, they are going through a wrong path. Some people sit and pray for hours to ask God to give them something. All they need is to let their internal Godliness or consciousness to work through them so they could reach to their goals not to ask an artificial concept to give them something.

The main responsibility of human being as related to the wrong doings of mental self is to be able to sacrifice the mental self and free self from the bondage and the dark prison of mental system. We see the example of sacrificing mental self in the story of Abraham trying to sacrifice his son Ismael. The information we get from Koran, Moslem holy book and the Bible, tells us that Abraham experiences a dream that he is sacrificing his son, Ismael. When he wakes up, he tries to follow what he was told by God or consciousness. But suddenly a lamb arrives and Abraham sacrifices the lamb instead of Ismael. Rumi tells us that we all have to sacrifice our mental selves. Thus we have to cut the head of three major deficiencies that include mental self, greed and stupidity. The word Islam means peace and surrendering to absolute reality and truth and the word Moslem means one who becomes one with his/her internal God, sacrifices his/her mental self, accept and surrender to consciousness and is at peace with self, others and society. Mansour Hallaj, a Persian humanist, philosopher, and mystic, several hundred years ago declared that he was truth and consciousness and asked people to kill his mental self. He was killed by the authorities of his time not understanding him and his humanistic ideas.

There are many religious concepts that have been misused particularly against members of religion other than our own. For example the concept of "Infidel" that member of one religion use against members of other religions and assign the wrong meaning or labels and try to demonize the members of other religion based on in-group and out-group mentality or deviant characteristic which is duality of mental system. To Rumi the word "infidel" represents being within the mental system and being attached and co-identified with the material world, thoughts, beliefs, and excitements. Thus, infidel means covering and hiding consciousness within and not recognizing or being aware of it. The word "dualism" is a mental concept which is characteristic of mental self, because mental self, having limited knowledge and using limited language has to compare two opposites or complementary things. Mental self, finds a partner for God that is a mental God. It can't comprehend unity of consciousness or God. The center of the circle of life is within human consciousness but not in the mental system.

The main mission of all religion which appeared in the world has been the same, to wake us up from our sleep within our mental system. Life and consciousness never sleeps. The religions that emerged as a means for a sacred end and purpose of creating unity among human beings and between humans and God or consciousness as well as waking us up from the deep sleep within our mental system, could not achieve its main purpose, because some interest groups either within the religion or within the state, deviated from the main direction and function of the religions which was creating unity among human beings and creating social justice, equality, democracy, freedom and independence. Instead, humans concentrating on the mental self, created conflict, division, wars of ideas and beliefs both between religions and within each religion among its sects. The ideological warfare converted to real wars that killed millions of people with the name of God and religions. While all human beings are representative of God in the form of consciousness within them they tried to go after a mentally constructed God that is not based on any reality but distortion of human thought and beliefs.

The real religion of every human being is the religion of humanism and appreciation of a high value of humanity as the center of the universe and understanding that all things have been created for human comfort, joy and happiness. We have our origin and the universal consciousness within us thus we don't need to search for the universal consciousness in the external world in in things, buildings, idols and places of worships although they have lower level of consciousness within them. As a consciousness we are all equal and we respect each other as such, thus there is no reason for any human to be enslaved by any other human. The surface differences of human being in their shape, heights, weights, appearances, race, ethnicity, culture and colors are just the temporary changing forms. What is eternal and essence of all human beings is the consciousness. We should free ourselves from the prison of our mental system and rejoin the universal consciousness.

Rumi believes that religious people who use their artificial and distorted mental selves live in their mental system and can only be aware of God or consciousness as a mental concept or mental God. These people experience continuous pain, suffering and negative excitements. However, people who are in love or lovers, they live in the realm of unity and experience the universal consciousness through love and spiritual attraction. These people experience love, tranquility, creativity in the realm of unity where it is always joy, party and relaxation. Their pray is their connectedness to the consciousness or God not to worship a mental God. Rumi believes that all people such as mystics and lovers who talk similarly is because they all have reached the treasure of presence and since there is only one universal consciousness they all speak from the same realm of unity. Those who have reached this kind of experience are flying like a bird freely in the space of unity and oneness and bring us the joy and happiness. Rumi states "What is to be done, O Moslems? For, I do not recognize myself. I am neither Christian, nor Jew, nor Gabr, nor Moslem." (Rumi, translated into English by Nicholson, 1868). What Rumi is trying to say is that we are not our labels or adjectives. We are not our religion, nationality, ethnicity, gender, etc. We are consciousness.

IX

Human's Place in the Universe

"Mystics consider perfect man as the main center of the world. Heaven and hell are considered as elements of the reality of perfect man and are respectively opposite to divine wrath and mercy. The reality and status of perfect man is above any form of thought or imagination, and is beyond the sphere of the thinking of regular human beings" (Dr. Safavi, 2009, P. 1)

Rumi believes that human is the center of the universe and has the picture and reflection of the universe within self and is a mirror and extension of universal consciousness. The whole world has been created for human joy, relaxation and happiness as well as freedom, independence and continuation of creativity. Thus, there is no reason for human to experience sadness, depression, oppression or being under the bondage of anything in this world. What is becoming depressed is not the universal consciousness within human but the trapped consciousness within the mental system by mental self that takes a form of physical consciousness and is constantly producing negative thought, beliefs, emotions, and unnecessary excitements. While our universal consciousness is unlimited, formless, timeless and eternal, our mental system and mental self is highly limited. Our real independence and freedom as human being is to be detached from any worldly ownership and material possessions and not to be addicted, co-identified or co-dependent on them. The worth of a man depends on the objects of his aspirations.

Rumi believes that the whole universe is in a state and process of becoming and being created. Everything is in constant motion and all the particles of the universe are vibrating and dancing and human as the highest level of consciousness is sharing the process of evolution and creation. However, after the evolution in the matter is completed in human form, in addition to the evolution of matter, the next major process of evolution occurs in human consciousness and human mind and there is no need for the matter to evolve any further. Every human as part of the universe has to be active, happy, joyful and creative and should be constantly dancing with the music of the universe. Each human is responsible for converting the energy of "to be" into the "act of to do" and "to become." consciousness gives us reviving vine of life, tranquility, and creativity, but gives our mental self, the bitter and sour taste of vinegar and a state of pain and suffering. Then, why should we complain when we are eternal like our source.

Rumi compares human existence with a night that has a full moon and reflects the light of consciousness to all the stars and planets. The night is symbolized as consciousness within the form, although the consciousness itself is formless and is the essence of life. A wonderful event has occurred and the consciousness going through solids, plants and animal arrived in the human physical and mental system and has created the human brain and mind. Thus, consciousness trapped within human system is an extension of God and consciousness. Tonight consciousness present and express itself through the human form. One of the stars or human says moon is with me tonight and consciousness manifest itself like a bright light. We are life and we are one with the whole life and feel a sense of unity with life and all humans. Moon is the symbol of us as humans. We are ascending to the moon so that material things of this world would not have access to us to pull us down. We make our root unlimited and experience the presence. The reason for tonight's party is that Consciousness wants to express itself through us. Thus, we pick flowers and drink the wine of life.

The caravan of humanity is on the path of awakening of mental selves and those who try to stop this caravan are not able to stop the caravan of consciousness. Human can reach to the unity of consciousness through four major dimensions: 1. Physical dimension, 2. Mental Dimension, 3. Excitements and emotion dimension and finally, 4. Spiritual dimension. The unity within the individual physical dimension can be obtained when all subsystem of the individual's physical dimension are coordinated and work parallel to each other as complementary part of human biological system. This can be achieved through physical consciousness and positive energy that provide a balance within the individual system. The mental dimension of human is composed of the mental system and the mental self which works within and through the mental system. The mental dimension reaches to a the state of unity when mental self tries to be calm and provide only the positive function of collecting information and create a complementary relationship with the social and physical environment. At any point our mental self has two forms of relationship with our social and physical environment. One is the physical and sensual relationship and the other is mental and comprehensive relationship. These two different ways of experiencing the external reality has to be matched and parallel to each other for us to be able to make correct sense of the external reality.

The third dimension which is our excitement and emotional dimension is under the control of our mental self which is addicted to pain and creates all kinds of negative and disturbing emotional state for us. In order to create unity within our emotional system and keeping our mental self, quiet, we should not impulsively react to any event, incident, condition or situation. The best approach is trying to relax without any reaction or judgement. The fourth dimension is our spiritual dimension which is under control of our consciousness and constantly tries to pull us out of our mental system the center of all types of pain and suffering. Our universal consciousness works constantly on all of our four types of dimensions as an unlimited energy. Our responsibility and obligation is to accept the reality of all situations and surrender to the universal consciousness. In this case instead of our mental self, working through us, the universal consciousness will lead us to through the right path to become unified with our origin.

Rumi believes that all parts of the universe are interconnected and share a common denominator of consciousness and energy with love and attraction as the major cement of the universe. Thus, nothing in the world is separate from other things or other parts of the universe. Before the creation of the universe, the evolution of everything including solids, plants, and animals were toward the existence of human being. But after creation of human being the evolution of the matter stopped and evolution continues within human mental system toward the universal consciousness. Along with the evolution of human mind and mental system, society also evolves to a highest level of social evolution. The path toward perfection is only possible in human societies through the evolution of consciousness. Both The sun and the mood are considered by Rumi as symbols of Light and consciousness which energizes all beings. But sometimes Rumi considers the Sun a symbol of consciousness and the moon a symbol of Hunan being.

The main challenge for us as human is to resolve the internal conflict we feel between the evil mental self and our real, objective self or consciousness. This conflict exist only within our mental system which works based on duality of life and comparing opposites such as good or bad; light or darkness; evil and angel; peace or war; love and hate, etc. at all times. We can resolve this problem by self-recognition, self-knowledge and self-awareness regarding our internal world. If we do not try to resolve this problem, then, we will suffer within a fantasy world with a feeling of emptiness and emotional psychological pain. However, when we burn the pains of the mental self and all the worldly attachments with the fire of love that comes from our consciousness, we receive the light of presence. We become unlimited space of acceptance, love and tranquility. To talk with the mental self is against the law of life and living and is not connected to life. Event of this moment is the essence of this moment, but we are not events and do not get attached to them or try to obtain a sense of identity from them. We should accept the life of this moment as it is and move parallel to it.

The major plan of life is for us to recognize and become aware of our con-sciousness as an extension of universal consciousness and appreciate ourselves as such. Thus we should let our universal consciousness to work on and through us and lead us through the path of perfection and help us to rejoin to our origin. But our responsibility is to cut the cord that attaches us to the worldly material and non-material things and distractions. Every attachment has to be recognized and thrown away one by one and one vat a time to make this conversion possible and faster. We should be able not to resist or fight against this process and go with the flow of life forces that through the dance of the universe will rejoin us to our source. The same way that the light of the sun radiates and change the stone into the jewels of different kind, the ray of light of the consciousness which touches our body and soul will turn and convert us to the universal consciousness. All of these conversions become possible through the love and unifying process of consciousness. If consciousness would not vibrate within every particle of our body we could not have any relationship with the external world.

Rumi encourages all human beings to search for consciousness within their selves, but not out there in the external world. Thus, knowing our real essence we will know our origin as consciousness. According to Rumi, knowing is a form of consciousness not a thought or belief. Consciousness will lead the way and send the knowledge through us to the world. Knowledge is within us we don't need to gain it from outside world. We should only experience the external world. However to understand is a thought process or belief. We have been conditioned to see the world through our mental system using mental pictures. There is no real life in the objects but within us. There are motions and vibration of energy within objects but not a conscious living life of human beings. Thus we should not search for the source of life giving consciousness in the external world or even in Kaaba or places of worships which are physical places. The beloved is not in the solid forms, places or time, but within our real selves at this moment.

To Rumi, love is the main motivational force to unite us with our origin and it is the cement of the universe which keeps every particles of the universe together. Love is a vibration of energy or consciousness that is aimed toward the beloved and all love toward anything in this world is really aimed toward the direction of the universal consciousness that attracts all forms of energy toward itself, the main source of energy. Knowledge of the heart or love is preferable to academic knowledge. Intense love of God or consciousness puts reason to silence and also puts an end to all thinking and arguments. Philosophers deceive themselves and are busy with concepts and are drowned in their arguments and reason and their philosophical speculation confuse us and do not provide us with the real knowledge and wisdom of consciousness. As human being we are encouraged by Rumi, to seek awakening of our spiritual senses through relaxation, tranquility, patience, acceptance and surrendering to the absolute reality or universal consciousness. Our spiritual senses are positioned within us as part of the consciousness trapped within our physical biological system. The main purpose of the existence of human is experiencing life, relaxation, acceptance, surrendering and experiencing presence of consciousness. We need to be informed and aware of the events only as observers without showing any impulsive reaction, judgement, and fighting against those events.

Rumi calls human as the flying birds of the day and mental self as the bird of the night or bat that only flies in the dark space of the mental system. The bird of the day is the emancipated consciousness and the bird of the night is physical and mental consciousness. To Rumi this world is a place of sleep and we should be careful not to go into a deep sleep. We are made of the materials and non-materials of the two worlds. One is our physical world and our body and mental system which are forms and the other one is our spiritual essence or consciousness which is formless, timeless and eternal. Human is simultaneously animal and rational soul, spirit and flesh or physical body. Everything in the universe works hand in hand to complete the creation of human being with all his/her dimensions. Rumi gives human a very high status and explain God and consciousness with human and through human. God and consciousness resides within us in the state of light system of energy and can stay in all forms without exception. We can't love both worlds at the same time the same way that a man can't love two women at the same time.

This person is fooling self, try to justify his wrong state. There are a lot of wrong concept we use to justify our wrong doings. Examples are reputation, jealousy, grandiosity, narcissism.

Rumi believes that organization comes from disorganization, population comes from being scattered all over, being one piece comes from breaking into pieces, intension comes from un-intention and finally existence comes from non-existence or nothingness. Thus real existence is non-existence of mental system. Organization comes from the destruction of mental self. A sense of existence is not in mental system but in nothingness. A tailor has to cut the clothes into several pieces, which is an act of destruction and then, puts and sews those separated parts together and create a new dress, an act of organization. When wheats or other seeds are grinded, an act of destruction occurs, but when it is turned into flour and a piece of bread is produced, it is an act of wholeness or organization. When a carpenter cuts the wood into pieces and then put those pieces together to make furniture, again an act of destruction and reconstruction occurs. Thus, integration and harmony comes from a chaotic situation. A real independence comes from the destruction of dependency and codependency.

Laws of Life and Consciousness Extracted from Rumi's Ideas

As human we are a loving being. To feel oneness is to be in love with the lover or origin. The concept of paradise based on the beauty of the worldly matters is promising but the real paradise is the realm of unity and presence of consciousness. In the world of unity only God is governing and the laws of life are our guidelines to follow. The laws of life and consciousness are also eternal and irreversible. Some of the laws of life extracted from Rumi's ideas include:

The Law of eternity: That as universal consciousness we are everlasting and eternal and never really die or perish although our physical body and mental system is perishable.

The Law of gratitude and appreciation: This law of life is based on the assumption that we are the same essence as the universal consciousness and life and appreciate the comfort of life, and abundance.

The Law of perfection and completeness: As universal consciousness we are perfect and complete. Thus, we do not need the mental system and mental self to work hard and try to reach to the perceptual perfection that is only a mental concept.

The Law of death and destruction: Based on the laws of life, it is our mental system and mental self with their thought, beliefs, opinions, customs, rites, excitements, emotions as well as anything material such as our physical body and material world that is artificial, deficient, temporary and transitory.

The Law of Acceptance and Surrender: We as human should accept any upcoming event, incident, situation or condition and surrender to the universal consciousness without any judgement, resistance or reaction.

The Law of Zeal and Enthusiasm: Universal consciousness is stranger to the internal mental system and mental self and, hides its essence from the established mental system and mental self.

The Law of Recognition and awareness of our Mental System and Mental Self: We are encouraged to become aware of evilness of our mental system and artificiality of our mental self, because awareness of this deficiency is equivalent of our freedom from the mental system and mental self.

The Law of quietness: As an extension of universal consciousness we should not engage in a repetitive, perseverative thoughts and talks. Because talking and thinking constantly is only activate the mental system and mental self and maintains it.

The Law of Stability and Tranquility: The universal consciousness is stable within us and is with us from the time of being in our mother's womb up to the time of death of our physical body and mental system and self.

The Law of Meaning and Formlessness: The universal consciousness is formless, faceless and immaterial. The realm of consciousness is the space of unity, spirituality, meaning and tranquility.

The Law of Timelessness of Consciousness: The universal consciousness does not exist in the psychological time of the past or future which, are only artificial concepts with no reality basis. The universal consciousness always is present at this moment which helps us to become one with it through the limitless and eternal space of this moment.

The law of Guidance: The universal consciousness is leading and guiding us at all times and attract us toward the oneness and unity by constantly working through us. Thus, we should let consciousness work through us at all times.

The Law of the evolution of consciousness within all forms: Consciousness is constantly in the process of evolution and this process started occurring and transferring through solids, plants and vegetation, animals and human being. However, the evolution of consciousness in human occurs at a higher level and when the consciousness goes into our mental system and establishes our mental self which experiences the external world through our physical senses, nerves, brain, cognition, thought, beliefs, opinions, customs, rites, and excitements and then, free itself by rejoining the universal consciousness. This is the highest evolution of the consciousness to go back to its origin.

The Law of the Function of Mental System and Mental Self and Freedom of the Consciousness from the Mental System: Our physical mental consciousness which is entrapped within our mental system finally jumps out of our mental system and mental self, creating excessive pain and sufferings which forces our physical mental consciousness becomes free from the prison of our mental system and dissolves our mental self.

The Law of Dooms Day or Latter Day: The universal consciousness operates from within all human beings and leads them to the point of the deactivating, destruction and dissolving their mental system and mental self which occurs within the life of this moment at any moment. The dooms day or latter day of each human being occurs separately based on each person's experience, action and level of maturity.

The Law of unlimited knowledge and wisdom of the universal consciousness: The universal consciousness is knowledgeable and aware of every form and events or incidents in the world, because it penetrates within any existing form and sees the world through their eyes with their experiences.

The Law of Sincerity of promises: The universal consciousness that penetrated within the forms of human beings who reached a high level of presence and enlightenment such as prophets or many mystics, and the promises that was provided by those elites indicates that universal consciousness provided us everything in abundance and made available all the necessary items needed for all the creatures of the universe.

The Law of Patience: In order to gain anything we have to be patient and wait for it. When we plant the seeds or a small tree, it takes a long time to grow and to become productive and for trees to bear fruits and for wheat to produce hundreds of seeds for one seed that we cultivated.

The Law of Presence: All creatures will reach to the stage of presence when the time is right and ripe and this is the last part of the evolution of consciousness in all forms.

The Law of Compensation: For everything we obtain, we have to give or sacrifice something as an exchange. In order to convert from our mental self and to become united with our real self or consciousness, we have to sacrifice our mental self. Nothing comes easy, we have to work hard to enjoy the product of our hard work.

The Law of Universal Love: All the particles of the universe are in a state of love and attraction and inter-connected and inter-related by the invisible force of energy and the universal consciousness that resides within them. Love is the unifying factor and the cement of the universe.

The Law of Commitment and Coordination: We have a deep commitment to become one with the universal consciousness and there is no other choice for us.

The Law of Attraction of the same essence: We have tendency to be attracted to the people who have something in common with us. If we have the integrity, sincerity and authenticity as our major traits, then we go after people who have the same type of trait. However, if we have pain and evilness of our mental self, glorified in us, we go after other mental selves who have similar trait. People who have reached the treasure of presence will go after people who have the same characteristics.

The Law of The Group: When a group of people engage in certain behavior, individuals blindly imitate or copy the group behavior thinking that if group does it must be right. Sometimes the group may engage in appropriate behavior, but a lot of times group may engage in destructive behavior. Thus, since group does it does not make it ok for individual to blindly imitate and do the same thing.

The law of No Reaction: To react impulsively toward any event, incident, situation or condition, would causes conflict, pain and sufferings. Events, incidents, situations or conditions are not positive or negative. They are neutral unless we use our mental system and mental self to define those events as terrible or harsh and then impulsively react to the negative situation as we perceive it.

X

Conclusion and Recommendations

*"The bird is flying high, and its shadow is speeding on the
earth, flying like a bird:
Some fool begins to chase the shadow, running (after it) so far
that he becomes powerless (exhausted), not knowing that it is
the reflection of that bird in the air, not knowing where is the
origin of the shadow. He shoots barrows at the shadow; his
quiver is emptied in seeking (to shoot it): The quiver of his life
became empty. His life passed in running hotly in chasing of the
shadow. (But) when the shadow of God is his nurse, it delivers
him from (every) phantom and shadow. The shadow of God
is that servant of God who is dead to this world and living
through God (Rumi, 13th Century, Mathnawi, I, 417-423)
Translated by Nicholson, 1925).*

The spiritual goal of Rumi involves deactivating, dissolving and weakening of
the mental self or ego (the shadow, artificial and temporary being) to the point
of relative selflessness, in order to reach to the state of enlightenment at this
moment or the "here and now" what he calls treasure of presence. The main
prophets such as Zoroaster, Moses, Jesus, Mohammad and Buddha emphasized on the weakening and suppressing our internal ego in order to reach the
presence or to the point of awakening and enlightenment. They were symbols of light, treasure of presence and enlightenment. Zoroaster the Persian
prophet introduced the concepts of "Ahura mazda," light and brightness (God

or consciousness) and "Ahriman," darkness (evil) as well as the concept of "Paradise" and "Hell" five thousand years ago. To Rumi, all of the people who awakened to and rejoined the universal consciousness and the enlightenment declared that they were nothing but consciousness within forms and tried to teach all other human beings that they have the same essence and existence and are made of consciousness. Rumi believes that "to be" is a given phenomenon, but "to become" is the main responsibility and struggle for human being because human has the power of consciousness within him/her to create. Light does not exist only outside our physical system, it is also resides within our physical system.

All enlightened people came and declared that they are of the same essence and existence as all other human beings are, but they had the opportunity to reach and become aware of the universal consciousness within them. They also indicated that we are not our body and mental system but consciousness which is using our body and mental system as a temporary vehicle and place of residence of our universal consciousness. We should become more than our physical body, mental self and mental system. This can be achieved through awareness and trying to reach to the enlightenment. There is only one universal consciousness within all creatures including human beings and that is the main agent of unity and common denominator of all living and non-living things. Our heart must be clear from forms and luxuries and other material and non-material belongings and instead to be full of formlessness, unlimited space and eternal light and treasure of presence. We should not worship the material objects and worldly things and instead to be aware of the consciousness within us. Thus if we are going to worship anything it is our formless, timeless, eternal consciousness not our body, mental system, thoughts, beliefs and excitements.

Rumi believes that when part of our universal consciousness goes into our mental system and creates mental physical consciousness and through life experiences this consciousness becomes mature and experienced, then time comes for our physical mental consciousness to rejoin the universal consciousness or the treasure of presence. However, this can be achieved only when our mental self is deactivated, dissolved and weakened and that we have suffered enough through constant pain that we experience that we will finally be willing to voluntarily free ourselves out of the mental system. Consciousness only temporarily stays in the forms including human body to experience the external world through human physical body, senses, and metal system. However, staying in the forms is temporary as long as body and mental system are functional. When the body and along with it the mental system dies, the consciousness leaves the body and rejoin the universal and consciousness. But it is also possible for consciousness that is trapped in the mental system by mental self, to jump out of the mental system and rejoin the total consciousness while we are still alive.

Rumi believes that when we sleep, we rejoin the universal consciousness and we become separated from our mental system and when we are dreaming, it is the universal consciousness that is active and aware of everything in the world and it is the same consciousness that is dreaming, not our mental self. By experiencing the temporary unification with our source or origin during each sleep and coming back to our mental system during our awake-time, the total consciousness prepares us for the final rejoining process of becoming one with our origin. To experience the unity we have been waiting for during all our life evolving as consciousness going through solids, plants, animals and human being and finally into the mental system, our last residence is the mental and physical system, before reaching to the level of enlightenment and treasure of presence. Thus every night we sleep, our consciousness or spirit gets out of our mental system and reaches the treasure of presence which is our origin. This is a practice and exercise of our physical mental consciousness to reach temporary unity with our source, the universal consciousness.

According to Rumi the most important need of human being is overcoming the separation from the source and freeing the consciousness by using love as a power to get out of the lonely state and place human has within the mental system. Rumi's suggestions and the solution to escape our misery and feelings of guilt, self-blames, self-put down, depression, sadness and feeling low, greed, fear, jealousy and many other negative feelings is to escape from the center of evil or mental self and rejoin our source or origin which is the universal consciousness. We should always live at present and seize the moment, because it is only life of this moment that is real, not life in the future or the past which are only mental concepts created by mental self or ego. Acceptance of the contemporary situations, conditions and events of this moment, eliminates unnecessary reactions and the corresponding negative consequences. To eliminate conflict, pain and suffering among people, we should throw away our shallow and surface differences that relate to our forms and appearances and instead to concentrate on the reality of oneness and unity of our total consciousness that exist within all forms and spaces including human beings. There is only one consciousness in the world.

According to Rumi, We should not react impulsively to any life situation, condition or event. Instead, we should take our time to process the information, analyze it, and make the right decision and take the best possible course of action. We should not define any situation, condition or event in a negative way. Because no situation, condition or event is negative unless we define it in a negative way and then react to it accordingly. People will cause social conflict with other people by impulsively reacting to different situations which creates emotional psychological and mental pain. Rumi's emphasize on being non-reactive and patient in any situation and giving it sometimes to analyze the situation is very similar to the concept of the "definition of the Situation", by W. I. Thomas, the American Sociologist. Thomas believed that, if men defines situation as real, they are real in their consequences. According to Thomas, "Preliminary to any self-determined act of behavior there is always a stage of examination and deliberation which he calls it "the definition of the situation" (Thomas 2002).

Mental self always thinks about the past or future and creates an intense chronic pain for us. We should forget about the past events, beliefs, thoughts and excitements. If we wish to think about the past, it should be only a way of learning from our past mistakes and experiences but not to be sorry or sad about what has happened. Thinking about the past event makes us depressed in two ways. One is thinking about the negatively perceived events which open the wounds of the old horrible events and two, is remembering and missing the good old days. Similarly thinking about future which is unknown and unreal and is only a concept, we develop anxiety and worries. It is only this moment which is the infrastructure of our life and the time of becoming one with our consciousness through the uniting factor of unconditional love. Within the mental system and colorful form, we are under bondage of colors, pictures, reflections, and other forms. Colors, forms, pictures and reflections are related to our thought, speech, arguments, verbal quarrels, beliefs, and excitements which are sign of a mental self, fighting with another mental self. However, our real objective, spiritual self is colorless, formless, unlimited and eternal.

Rumi is using the analogy of a buzzing sound of the bees to reflect the perseverative parroting of the mental system and mental self which can't be relaxed at any time. We should keep our talkative mental self, quiet and prevent it from engaging in racing thought processes. We usually either engage in perseverative thought process or perseverative verbal conversation that is considered vocal thinking. Perseverative thought process and talking creates stress, anxiety and irritability, and as a consequence distract us and divert our attention from the main objective we may wish to achieve. This harmful mental activity does not let us concentrate on our tasks and we may not be able to experience relaxation at any moment. We should relax and concentrate on positive aspects of our life and stay away from negative thought processes. The best solution to any negatively perceived event or incident is to accept the event or incident without any judgement and let go of the event. Human has the unlimited potential and capacity of reaching the highest level of freedom and independence within self, nature, society and the world by freeing self from the limiting factors of this world.

According to Rumi, our mental self is always in a rush to do things due to the mentality that good thing comes in the future, we should be able to control our mental self or ego and do not let our ego rush us in doing things. By rushing into doing something without using our real, spiritual self we will not be able to preplan our activities based on accurate data and information, thus, we will experience the negative consequence of our impulsive behavior. We should fly like a humming bird, drinking the natural sweet syrup of the flowers while flying and not to sit on them, getting attached to and becoming co-identified with them. If a bird stay in one place for a long time, become attached to it, forgets the art of flying and behaves like a mouse living in a small hole and being afraid to get out of a house made of dirt. To experience the state of eternal existence, we should never become attached to anything in the external world which is temporary and perishable. Rumi considers the unity as the main order of the whole existence and sees all the opposites, contrasts and differences within the framework of unity and believes that all the dualities, contrasting, and conflicting phenomena will end up with unity which is the essence of the whole universe and that also shows that everything is directed to the same source of existence.

Rumi recommends that if someone who has a strong sense of mental self or evil and tries to fight and cause conflict with you, it is better to ignore, stay away or not to fight back. Reduce the resistance to his/her behavior to zero and do not put fuel over their fires. Acceptance of existing situation or condition will reduce our resistance to a very low level, thus, we do not need to show any reaction to someone else's behavior. In fact, we should not let other people to decide how we will behave. If we behave by showing reaction every time, then people with strong mental selves can play with us like toys and we will dance to their wrong music. We should concentrate on our real self by being satisfied, with no greed of any kind, accept our life situations, conditions, events and incidents without any judgement and resistance and to surround ourselves to the universal consciousness and the treasure of presence which provides us with real tranquility and helps us to be at peace with ourselves and others.

We should constantly and actively observe our own behavior and action and pay attention to our physical, emotional, psychological and spiritual dimensions. Conscious observation helps us to observe and identify our mistakes, limitations, and shortcomings. We should concentrate on ourselves not others and should not try to change others because we think they are wrong and we are right. We as human beings possess two types of consciousness. One form of our consciousness is our temporary, artificial mental self-consciousness, which includes mental, physical, material, formal consciousness. The other form is the real objective consciousness which is unlimited, eternal, formless, life consciousness which relates to our origin and essence. After our physical mental self-consciousness is matured and experienced within our mental system, it becomes one with our real, objective consciousness. This conversion from the evil of mental self and the hell of mental system into becoming one with universal consciousness and light is not a theory but a practical matter. Mental self and mental system being temporary and only reflection of the universal consciousness only helps us to relate to our external world, while, the universal consciousness is the essence and the origin of our existence. Thus, the light as energy is the same as consciousness and wherever we see life or a living thing, we are experiencing consciousness in different forms.

The final goal of the evolution of consciousness after being matured in our mental system is to reach to the real enlightenment, freedom and the treasure of presence. However, this goal can be achieved through the production of physical, emotional, psychological and mental pain and being born and free from the darkness of mental system and being tired of all those pains related to different aspects and dimensions of external world and the related distractions of our mental self. However, this can also be achieved through a high level of patience, acceptance of the existing reality and surrendering ourselves to the total consciousness. The direction of the evolution of the universal consciousness is a long and continuous move from self- alienation and previous separation toward rejoining and becoming one with the universal consciousness. Evolution of consciousness is also a move from the realm of determinism, bondage and imprisonment of consciousness within the matter and mental system toward a realm of freedom and independence of human being from the bondage. Rumi also considers the evolution of consciousness in human being a freedom from the attachment to the time, location, land, family, and any other worldly things.

Rumi believes the whole world of existence is universal light, energy and consciousness and the universal sound is the sound of the dance of the forms and movement of all forms toward their origin to achieve unity. Thus the sound and music of the universe is the music of oneness. The main type of evolution is slow and gradual quantitative change of the different parts of the universe and finally, a sudden qualitative change that comes out of a revolutionary change in the changeable parts. An individual, society and the whole universe is in a constant state of flux and change toward a higher quality of life and existence. Everything came out of nothingness and everything goes back to nothingness. To become one with universal consciousness one should become selfless, thus, we should dissolve our mental self. The external world is like a form over the spiritual world that is like a sea of unity. Our universal consciousness constantly and repeatedly sends fire and sparkles of awakening and tries to dissolve our mental self, but mental self, ignore the message until there would not be any choices left except surrendering to absolute reality of universal consciousness.

In this world we go through two major types of experience and being temporarily imprisoned in two different places of residence. When we come to this world we have to stay in two different wombs and be born twice. Once we are developed in our mother's womb and born to this world. The second time we have to grow and develop within our mental system through our mental self, interacting with this world until we are ready and mature enough to be born again from our mental system into the world of unity and universal consciousness which is the realm of formlessness, timelessness, eternal and unlimited space. In the mother womb, it is the mother that feels all the pain and when the pain become too intense for the mother to bear it and when we have become mature and developed enough, we are born into this world. But the second time, it is our mental self that is causing the intense pain and suffering for us and our physical consciousness that we have no choice but being born again and jumping out of the womb of our mental system. The same way that after we are born from our mother's womb, we should not be attached to the cord where we used to receive our food and oxygen and should adapt to the new climate of this world and receive our food, water and oxygen from the world, we should not be attached to our mental system and mental self and should cut the cord not only with the mental system but with the external world and try to adapt to the new climate and space of unity of the universal consciousness.

Rumi believes that from the solids through plants, animals and human we are nothing but consciousness and even as a human we have all forms and scars of solid, plant, animal and human consciousness within us. Thus, the biggest sin is becoming co-identified and attached to the worldly things including our mental system and working through it. Because becoming co-identified with our mental system, thought, beliefs, opinions, excitements and material things including our body, keeps us in the dark and being in the sleep of the mental system. To Rumi, all lives are interrelated and have the common denominator of consciousness within them. Rumi believes that the story of Adam and Eve (symbol of first human beings) and their major sin they have committed was becoming co-identified and attached to their mental system and used their mental self for the first time to see the external material world through the eyes of mental self. For Eve to eat the "apple" or "wheat" as the symbols of external material world, and asking Adam to do so, they become attached to the worldly things. Due to becoming co-identified with the mental system, developing mental self, Adam engaged in the first cognitive distortion of blaming Eve for his action of listening to Eve and eating the same fruit or seed. This act was the first human step toward freedom of choice and engaging in a research to find out about the nature of something new.

The best way to save humanity from self-destruction is for human beings to realize that they all are consciousness in different forms and that consciousness is the essence of all life forms and common denominator of all the particles of the universe. Thus, the unity is an objective phenomenon and it comes from power of life, love and consciousness. Unity at macro level comes from variety and differences of the constituent parts. Thus people of different cultures, nations, races or ethnicity are all united through their internal consciousness which is the same consciousness. Their differences and varieties make life interesting for all people. The same way that we have different kinds of flowers with different shapes colors, designs, and fragrances, we have different varieties of trees and animal, we also have humans that are only different on their appearances. Another important point to consider is that we should let consciousness within us to work through us and lead us toward a productive, joyful and successful life and do not let our evil mental self to keep us in the hell within which is our mental system.

Rumi provides many specific recommendations to consider for a healthy and productive life:

1. We should always be open to learning and consider ourselves student of life up to the last day of our physical mental life.
2. We should constantly strife and work hard to recognize and reach to the wisdom and knowledge of the universal consciousness which is inherent in us.
3. We should always search for truth and a real meaning in our life.
4. We should correctly research and recognize all phenomena within the external world instead of blindly accepting any information about anything.
5. We should know and love our real self instead of being slave of our mental self is based on selfishness and hates self and others. Love is answer to all human miseries. The survival of human species is based on love. Without love, people develop hate based on their mental selves and destroy the world by wars and different forms of human mass destruction.
6. We should not be unidimensional and stay away from any forms of biases, discrimination, prejudice, relating to other people around us.
7. We should understand that everything in the universe is relative except the universal consciousness.

8. We should be aware of our internal world and adapt it to the phenomena of the external world and the universe.

9. We should be able to distinguish between the stepwise experiences and the experience of synchronicity and be aware of the importance of the time of this moment which is eternal.

10. We should be able to distinguish between our limited mental system and the related thought, belief, opinion, reason, logic and excitement and our unlimited real essence.

11. We should turn and convert our "To be," into "To become" and "To do" or achieve self-actualization which is the major responsibility of every human being.

12. We should understand that every byproduct of our mental system and mental self is nothing but a thought concept which is different from the real experience and action.

13. We should reach to a level of humanity that we are able to control our mental self or ego and all of our primitive animal and human instincts.

14. To be aware of unconditional love and see, feel and love the universal consciousness in everything and everyone and to recognize the unity of consciousness within all forms including human beings.

15. Never emphasize on the difference between the "I" and the "He/She" or "We" and "Them." Because this is a way of duality of our mental system and mental self to separate self from others so that he/she can have opportunity to cause conflict, resistance and fights.

16. Do not react, prejudge or judge. Accept every incident, event, situation or condition without any judgement or showing any reaction. This is a way of staying calm and relaxed.

17. Do not try to understand everything through the limited and biased knowledge and logic of our mental self. Because the real understanding and knowledge comes from our universal consciousness.

18. We should resolve the problem of the death by understanding that nothing really dies. and mental system becomes deactivated and our physical body becomes dissolved and transforms to smaller parts and creates many new forms of lives and our consciousness trapped within

our physical mental system will be released and rejoin the universal consciousness. Life and death are not really different in essence but only in situations very similar to the river and the sea or ocean. Because both are waters but one in constant motion and struggle to reach its origin that is the sea or the ocean.

19. We should be honest with ourselves and accept our own mistakes so that we would not make the same mistake over and over. Making mistakes is a way of learning the right thing.

20. We should have self-confidence, self-respect and positive self-expression and attitude toward our real self. If we are not able to respect ourselves, we will not be able to respect others.

21. We should love everybody and everything. Love is more powerful than the reason and logic.

22. We should have a real sense of empathy and sympathy with all other creatures.

23. We should maintain a major principle in our life.

24. Patience and acceptance along with surrendering to consciousness and going with the flow of life, and not swimming against the current will provides us with an ability to tolerate any difficult and harsh incident, event, situation, or condition and helps us to reach to our treasure of presence.

25. We should concentrate on producing, organizing and creating useful things and situations instead of destroying things.

26. We should be merciful and kind toward other human beings instead of being revengeful and holding grudges.

27. Leading, teaching and helping others instead of breaking or defeating others.

28. We should always try to maintain the justice by not oppressing, exploiting, and controlling other people.

29. We should consider everyone equal in their values and existence as human beings.

30. We should strive to obtain freedom and independence but not to the point of becoming unleashed and destroying others.

Rumi tells us that we should be naked and not to hide ourselves under a cover or mask. We should try to present our self to other people as we are not as whom we want them to think we are. Thus we should not try to play role, impress others and obtain attention. If we try to be our real self, then there is no need to spend a lot of energy to show who we are not. Hiding self from others is the activity of our mental self, because mental self always think he/she is deficient and incomplete, thus tries to hide his/her self. To Rumi the main problem arises when we are not aware of our real self or our origin forgetting that we are consciousness not our body or mental self. Thus, we should try to throw away, our covers and masks, and all the unnecessary material and non-material belongings that we are hiding behind. People are so worried and anxious to present themselves as somebody else or what they are not that they forget who they really are.

Rumi calls us and tell us that as conscious human being we are responsible to experience the formlessness, timelessness and nothingness without mental system and mental self. We should live at this moment and at any moment we should be aware and conscious of our internal God or consciousness. We should not forget who we really are. Within the life of this moment time and space become unified. We should be observer and helper of this process. If we understand that we are not limited to time or space, we would not be afraid of the death of our body and mental system, because we have consciousness of eternal life. We are made up of life and consciousness. If we become aware of our unlimited root, we will also become aware of our unlimited space. Events and incidents are occurring and dying, but it is always the life of this moment that is present. Thus, we can never really become separated from the life of this moment.

Some Symbolic Vocabularies used by Rumi (13th Century)

Abraham = A symbol of consciousness.

Adjectives = Labels, position, status, privilege, wealth, education, co-identification, Codependency, attachment.

Aghsa Mosque = Human heart.

Ahriman = Evil. (This word was used by Zoroaster).

Ahura mazda = God or consciousness. (This word was used by Zoroaster).

Awakened = Separated from mental system, enlightened,

Awakened Zuleika = Zuleika (wife of the prime minister of Egypt) got her spiritual vision back and reached the treasure of presence.

Bitter water = False consciousness of mental self.

Blind Zuleika = Blinded mental self.

Blood = Pain and suffering.

Body = Form, picture, material.

Breath of air = A moment, an instance.

Buddha = A symbol of consciousness.

Burning = the process of purification of the soul.

Cat = A symbol of death.

Characteristics of Mental Self = Negative thought, beliefs, opinions, excitements, negative emotions, greed, jealousy, anger, aggression, fear, anxiety, sadness, depression, blaming self and others, fault finding, un-satiated, desires and wants, vengefulness, grandiosity, low self-esteem, resistance, reactivity, attachment, codependency, co identification, suspiciousness, paranoia, un-trustfulness, duality, hate, conflict, contrast, fight

Chastity = An artificial concept, false identification.

Clothes = Frames of thoughts and beliefs.

Consciousness = God, energy, light, absolute spirit, formlessness, eternal, immaterial, clear water, cloud, fog, king, leader of orchestra, eternal color, real self, objective self, Industrious, origin, source, Pure light, clean and clear light, light of presence, Wine, Jacob, Abraham, Zoroaster, Moses, Jesus, Mohammad, Buddha, beloved, friend, bird of the sky, flower face,

Cow = A symbol of limitation of mental system.

Donkey = physical consciousness.

Down = Latter day.

Drunken = Drunken with the love of God or consciousness, drunken with the wine of ecstasy of the love of God or consciousness.

Duality = Mental self sees things as opposites such as day and night, good or bad, hot and cold.

Emerald = Becoming conscious and aware of life.

Evil eyes = Eyes of mental self.

Fire = pain, excitement, love.

Fly = thought, belief, excitement, event, incident, situation, condition, pain.

Forgiving = Work of real self or consciousness.

Formless wine = immaterial wine of life.

Frozen Python = Frozen mental self within mental self.

Head and head band = Reason.

Human = Lover, Sufi in search of the beloved, darvish, dervish, wind of morning, revolutionary, life energy, hunter, cup, boy, parrot, bird, Symorgh, Angha (mythological bird).

Infidel = (Kaffir) Sinner, covering the truth, unbeliever, Co-identified, attached, codependent with worldly material.

Jacob = A symbol of consciousness.

Jealousy = Comparison of two forms and characteristic of mental self.

Joseph = A symbol of consciousness, human who achieved treasure of presence.

Joseph wells = Wells of mental system, where Joseph's brother threw him in.

Khizer =- A symbol of consciousness, living life.

Killing = breaking one's attachment, co-identification and codependency with the mental self or ego.

Leafless leaf = voice of paradise.

Lily of the Valley = Flower with hundred language, soft talker.

Lion = Presence, human, God, consciousness, human.

Mental Self = Evil, demon, Satan, ego, golly, internal wolf (Tenacious), internal fox (deceitful), Joseph's brothers, pain, suffering, domineering self, Donkey (Ignorant trait), scorpion (Poisonous) snake, (Poisonous), dragon (dangerous), Bat, stove of a bath, old fox, sore, dirt, blind, deaf, thought, beliefs, opinion, Deviant, abnormal, inappropriate, deviant, ignorant, sick, form, picture, reflection, Transitory, artificial, distorted, co-dependent, co-identified, attached, ugly, bear, Stupid, blind mouse, double vision, raw, immature, uncooked, a sense of existence, Eater, being eaten, enemy within, bee, desert, bird of thought, sour, bitter.

Mental Self's Food = approval, attention, respect.

Mental System = Hell, prison, Dark place, cold place, Fire, trap of mental self, Jail, strange land, moon, thorn land, city, region, pan, resistance, fight and rage against life.

Mature = Fruitful consciousness, ready.

Messiah = A symbol of consciousness of presence, savior, Jesus.

Migration = Migrating from mental system to the realm of unity, travel, conversion.

Mirror = Clean and clear light of heart.

Mohammad = A symbol of consciousness.

Morning = Time of awakening and enlightenment.

Moses = A symbol of consciousness.

Moslem = a person who is peaceful and has been surrendered to God or consciousness.

Mud = Mixture of consciousness and mental self or mixture of water and dirt.

My property = A sense of ownership and the mental picture of self and belongings.

Nightingle = the bird of the night a symbol of the soul lounging toward the source.

Old = Past oriented and living in the past.

Poison = Pain of mental self.

Real Self = Consciousness, energy, light, angel (Pari), angelic soul.

Realm of Unity = the limitless universe of God or consciousness, Rose garden, nothingness, yield of life, original home, land of joy, this moment, ocean, sea, lake, sky, paradise and eternal beauty.

Reputation = an artificial concept, false identification.

Roof = Sky, realm of unity.

Rose garden = Rose garden of conscience and heart.

Rotation of time = Rotation of thought and beliefs within the mental system.

Self = Mental construct, mental reflection, mental picture, figment of our imagination.

Separation = Separation from the source or origin, God or consciousness.

Shiekh = Complete human.

Shore = Secure place.

Smell = Energy of the form.

Smoke = Form, picture.

Split pea = Raw and immature human.

Sugar = Joy, happiness, creativity, sweetness.

This world = Tabriz, Egypt, river.

This year = This moment.

Treasure of Presence = Consciousness without co-identification, codependency or attachment to time, location, thought, belief, opinion, excitement, and materialistic things.

Unclean = Attached, co-identified, codependent.

Untied nut = Dead mental self.

Village = A symbol of limited space.

Wine of the divine = Laws of life.

Work without pay = Wasting time, chewing gum, creating pain for self or others.

Youth = Future oriented and living in the future.

Zoroaster = A symbol of consciousness, the eternal or first light, old star.

Zuleika = Symbol of passion.

References

Beck, A. T (1999) Prisoners of Hate: the Cognitive Basis of Anger, Hostility and Violence. New York: Harper Collins

Beck, A. T (1976) Cognitive Therapy, Emotional Disorders. New York: International University Press.

Bruno, F. J. (1993) Psychological Symptoms. John Willey & Sons Inc., New York. Chichester. Brisbane. Toronto. Singapore

Cooley, Charles H. (1930). Self-Growth Out of a Person's Social Interaction with Others,

Descartes, R, (1979) Meditations on first Philosophy, Translated from the Latin by Donald A. Cress, Hackett Publishing Company, Inc.

Dollard & Miller, N. (1950) Personality and Psychotherapy. New York McGraw Hill.

Ellis, R. A. 1977) How to Live with and Without Anger, New York: Reader s' Digest Press.

Frankl, Victor E. (1998) Man's Search for Meaning. (Revised ed.) New York: Washington Square Press.

Freud, Z. (1923) the Ego and the Id, the Standard Edition with a Biographical Introduction by Peter Gay.

Fromm, Erick, (1983) For the Love of Life, Translated from the German By Robert and Rita Kimber, Edited by Hans Jurgen Schultz, The Free Press, A Division of McMillan, Inc. New York, NY.

Fromm, E. (1971) The Heart of Man: Its genius for good and evil. First Perennial Library Edition published.

Fromm, E. (1966) Psychoanalysis and Religion. Yale University Pres, New Haven.

Fromm, E. (1956) Art of Loving. Harper & Row Publishers, Inc., New York NY.

Goode, E. (1984) Deviant Behavior. Second Edition, Prentice Hall Inc., Englewood Cliffs. New Jersy.

Hawton, k., et al. (1989) Cognitive Behavior Therapy For Psychiatric Problems, A Practical Guide, Oxford Medical Publications, Oxford, Oxford University Press, New York, Tokyo.

Horney, K. (1950) Neurosis and Human Growth, Norton New York.

James, W. (1904) Does Consciousness Exist? Journal of Philosophy, Psychology and Scientific Methods, 1, 477-491. In Wallace B. & Leslie E. Fisher (1987, 1983) Consciousness and Behavior, Allyn and Bacon, Inc., Boston. London. Sydney. Toronto.

James, William. (1890) Jamesian Theory of Self, Wikipedia the free encyclopedia, in Principles of Psychology.

James, W. (1890) Principles of Psychology, Vol. 1, New York: Holt. In Wallace, & L. Fisher (1987, 1983) Consciousness and Behavior, Allyn and Bacon, Inc., Boston. London. Sydney. Toronto. B.

Kyokai, B. D. (1966, PP. 42, 43) Toppan Printing Company. (S) Pte. Ltd.

Mafi, M. & A. M. Kolin. (1999) Rumi, Whispers of the Beloved, Translated by Mafi & Kolin, Thorsons, An imprint of Harper Collins Publishers, (P. 48)

Maslow A. H. (1971) The Farther Reaches of Human Nature, A Viking Press Book.

McKay, M. R. P. D. & J. McKay (1989) When Anger Hurts: Quieting the Storm Within. New Harbinger Publications Inc., Oakland California.

Mead George H. (1934) Mind, Self and Society, edited and introduced by C. Morris. Chicago: Chicago University of Chicago.

Moshiri, Fereydoon. (2015) Selected Poems, Translated from Persian Language by Franak Moshiri.

Natsoulas, T. (1978a) Consciousness, American Psychologist, 33, 906-914.

Natsoulas, T. (1978b) Toward a Model of Consciousness in the light of B. F. Skinner's contribution. Behaviorism, 6, 139-176.

Nicholson, R. A. (1925) Translation of Rumi's Works, Mathnawi I, (417-423).

Peck M. Scott. , M. D. (1983) People of the Lie, the Hope for Healing Human Evil. A Touchstone Book, Published by Simon & Schuster, New York London Toronto Sydney Tokyo Singapore

Peck M. Scott., M. D. (1978) The Road Less Travelled. A New Psychology of Love, Traditional Values and Spiritual Growth, A Touchstone Book, Published by Simon & Schuster, New York.

Rotter, J. B (1982) the Development and Application of Social Learning Theory. New York. Praeger.

Rotter, J. B. (1981) the Psychological Situation of Social Learning Theory. In D. Magnusson (Ed.) Toward a Psychology of Situations: An International Perspective, Hillsdale, N. J.: Lawrence Erlbaum.

Rotter, J. B. (1954) Social Learning and Clinical Psychology. Prentice Hall, New York.

Rumi, Jalalaldin Mohammad Molavi. (1278) Mathnawi-ye Manawi (Spiritual Couplets), A six Volume Poem, "Konia Manuscripts" Published five years after Rumi's Death (Persian Language)

_____. (1278) Diwan-e-Shams-e-Tabrizi (Diwan-e- Kabir) "Konia Manuscripts," Published five years after Rumi's Death in Persian Language, named in honor of Rumi's master Shams.

_____. (1278) Fihi Mafih Provides a record of seventy one talks and lectures given by Rumi on various occasion to his disciples, In Persian Language. English translation was first published by A. J. Arberry as Discourses of Rumi, New York: Samuel Weiser, 1972. The translation of the second book by: Wheeler Thackston, Sign of the Unseen Putney, V T: Threshold Books, 1994.

Samenow, S. E. (1984) Inside Criminal Mind, Times Books, a division of Random House, Inc. New York, and simultaneously in Canada by Random House of Canada Limited, Toronto.

Shahbazi, Parviz. (2015, 2016). TV Program the "Treasure of Presence Programs."

Skinner, B. F. (1953) Science and Human Behavior, the Free Press. a Division of Macmillan Publishing Co. , Inc. New York (P. 284).

Skinner, B. F. (1971) Beyond Freedom and Dignity, a Bantum/Vintage Book, a Division of Random House. New York. (P. 190).

Thomas, W. I. (2002) the Definition of the Situation, in Self, Symbol, and Society: Classic Readings in Social Psychology, Nathan Rousseu (ed.), (Lanham, MD: Rowman & Littlefield) PP. 103-115.

Thomas, W. (1923) "The regulation of the Wishes," in the Unadjusted Girl with Cases and standpoint for Behavior Analysis, Boston: Little Brown & Company, 41-69.

Tussing, L (1959) Psychology for Better Living. John Willey & Sons, PP.316-323 in Cox, F. (1973). Psychology (Eds.) WM. C. Brown Company Publishers, Dubuque, Iowa, P. 474.

Wallace, B. & Leslie E. Fisher (1987, 1983) Consciousness and Behavior, Allyn and Bacon, Inc., Boston. London. Sydney. Toronto

Whinfield, E. H. (1898) "Masnavi e Ma'navi, the Spiritual Couplets of Moulana Jalalu-d-din Muhhamad Molavi Rumi," 6 Vol. Translated from Persian Language into English. Copy Right: Iran Chamber Society.

Yokelson, S. & Samenow, S. E (1976) the criminal personality, Vol. 1, II, and III: A Profile for Change. Jason Aronson Inc., Northvale, New Jersey London. (pp. 251-453).

Other Sources:

Aryan Pur-Kashani, A. (2004) the Pocket Persian English Dictionary, Sepehr Printing House.

Collins English Dictionary (2012), Digital Edition.

Danzinger, E. First Content editor for kabalaonline.org.

www.ingramcontent.com/pod-product-compliance
Lightning Source LLC
Chambersburg PA
CBHW071354280526
45787CB00001B/325